MW00856479

THE
CREATIVE
POWER
OF
THOUGHT

Other titles* in the

LIBRARY OF
HIDDEN KNOWLEDGE

The New Master Key System
The New Science of Getting Rich
Natural Abundance, Ralph Waldo Emerson's Prosperity
The New Game of Life and How to Play It
One Law, Henry Drummond on Nature and Love
As We Think, So We Are
The Spiritual Science of Emma Curtis Hopkins

---

*These titles are all published by Beyond Words/Atria, a division of Simon & Schuster, and may be ordered from their website: www.beyondword.com or anywhere books are sold.

THE
CREATIVE
POWER OF
THOUGHT

THOMAS TROWARD'S METAPHYSICS

modern interpretation by RUTH L. MILLER

LIBRARY OF
HIDDEN KNOWLEDGE

www.portalcenterpress.com

The Creative Power of Thought: Thomas Troward's metaphysics

© 2021 by Ruth L. Miller

Published by Portal Center Press
www.portalcenterpress.com

ISBN: 978-1-936902-42-2

With appreciation to Richard Cohn and Cynthia Black of Beyond Words Publishing who invited me to create the Library of Hidden Knowledge, interpreting the writings of the major contributors to the New Thought movement, the ideas of which are the basis for Rhonda Byrne's video and book, *The Secret*, and gave me permission to add to the series with another publisher.
- *rlm*

Printed in the U.S.A.

"New Thought is not the name of a particular sect, but is rather the essential factor for our individual development. Everyone who finds this new basis of thinking experiences the cosmos in a radically different way, for from this standpoint each of us is not just a part of the general effect, but part of the cause.

"This order of cause and effect, and this method of thinking, are not new. They are older than the foundation of the world, for they are those of the creative Spirit itself; and all through the ages this teaching has been handed down in various forms—the true meaning of which has been perceived by only a few in each generation."

~Thomas Troward, (The Hidden Power & Other Papers on Mental Science)

CONTENTS

ORIGINAL TEXTS

NOTE FROM THE EDITOR

Although not published by Beyond Words/Simon & Schuster, this book is really the last book in the series called the Library of Hidden Knowledge. It was begun in 2012, before that series was terminated by the publisher, and has been sitting on my computer, waiting for me to stop pastoring churches and devote the time it needed to be completed.

As such projects often do, it has morphed into a somewhat different text from the one I was working on then, but this new version is, perhaps, more relevant to the time in which we are now living.

The reason I have this time is the great "corona virus lockdown" of 2020. The whole world has set aside its normal values and ways of doing things in an attempt to stop the spread of a virus that baffles health care professionals in its inconsistencies and range of symptoms.

In a strange way, this time is therefore the perfect moment to immerse myself in the clear wisdom of this amazing man. His ideas, expressed in extremely lengthy sentences and paragraphs, are perfect capsules of the essential understandings that have become the basis of the New Thought movement. They have transformed lives for over a hundred years through Unity, Divine Science and Spiritual Living centers and churches, and have inspired the works of motivational teachers ranging from Napoleon Hill, Wallace Wattles, and Earl Nightengale to Rhonda Byrne in *The Secret*.

As with all the Library of Hidden Knowledge books, this one has two parts. The first part is my "translation," or interpretation, of the original writings from their Victorian prose into modern form and language, with summary points and exercises. This is followed by the author's original text. The hope is that you will go back and forth, using my work to help make sense of the original author's text, and using my exercises to help make the writer's points a part of your experience.

One more point: because each essay is a series of logical steps toward conclusions, I've taken the liberty of pulling his conclusions out into indented "quotes" to help the reader see them.

May Judge Troward's ideas be the inspiration that lifts you beyond the trials of the moment into the heights you were born to know.

Ruth L. Miller

INTRODUCTION

The Fascinating Life of Thomas Troward

Thomas Troward was born in the Punjab region of India in 1847. His father was a colonel in the British-Indian Army and the family was transferred to Ceylon (Sri Lanka) soon after Thomas' birth.

Like most children of the British Raj, Thomas grew up in a British compound with native servants and at age 11 was sent back to England to attend school, staying in that country with friends of the family during holidays. He is said to have been quiet and studious, preferring to read rather than play with other boys.

In 1865, at the age of 18, he graduated from college with honors in literature. Although at heart he always considered himself an artist and a painter, he accepted the advice of his elders to study Law.

On completion of preparation for the bar in 1869, at age 22, he took the Indian Civil Service Examination. One of the subjects was metaphysics, and Troward surprised everyone with his original answers. Schoolboys studied a particular form of metaphysics in those days and the answers he gave were not at all what he'd been taught.

In spite of this, he passed, so he married and returned to India with his new wife. He arrived as an aide and soon became an assistant commissioner. Then he was promoted to Divisional Judge in the Punjab, not far from where he was born. He served there for the next 25 years, adjudicating and mediating issues between people of many different religious and linguistic backgrounds, ranging from Muslim to Jew, Buddhist to Jain, Sikh to Christian, and several varieties of Hindu.

It's not too surprising, then, that he explored most of the world's spiritual traditions and had many paranormal experiences, some of which are described in his book, *The Law and the Word*.

Outside of spiritual study, Troward's greatest delight was painting. He won several prizes for art in India and his watercolors are still on display in a few museums in India and the U.K. There is a story that during World War I he was nearly arrested for setting up his canvas and paints on the Cornwall coast!

He and his wife had three children in India, whose childhoods were very like his own, living in the British compound with native Indians as servants and helpers. Sadly, his whole family took a fever and died, not long before he retired, in his late 40s.

In deep mourning he returned to England to build a new life. After a while he married a second time and had three more children, who grew up in the proper English middle-class fashion. In the foreword to a posthumous publication entitled, *Troward's Comments on the Psalms*, his second wife, Sarah Ann, writes:

> When he retired from the Bengal Civil Service in 1896, he decided to devote himself to three objects -- the study of the Bible, writing his books, and painting pictures... He believed that the solution to all our problems was there (in the Bible) for those who read and meditated with minds at one with its Inspirer.

As a properly educated English gentleman in the Civil Service, Troward could read the Greek and Latin of his school years as well as Biblical Hebrew and he learned the Arabic and Sanskrit scripts of India. He used this ability to thoroughly digest all of the sacred books of the eastern traditions, as well as the Bible and the Quran. Because of this extensive study and his experiences there, he became more and more convinced that there was a way to synthesize the essential points of the world's religions into one common approach to metaphysics.

In 1902, therefore, shortly after returning to England, he began to write for the British New Thought publication *Expressions*. He had already developed his philosophy of Mental Science when he was introduced to the "Higher Thought Center" of London through Alice Callow, who happened to meet him in a London tea room. There, the story goes, she was sitting across from him as he was writing on a tablet and "could not help but see" that what he was writing was "higher thought," to which he replied "I certainly hope so."

This group immediately recognized him as an extremely articulate and learned individual. He was invited to give a series of lectures and in 1904 delivered his famous Edinburgh lectures at Queens Gate in Edinburgh, Scotland. It was a very small but appreciative group, but, it is said that between his boring delivery and complex ideas, even this captive, willing audience hardly understood what he was saying. They would politely sit through the lecture, waiting with anticipation for the printed version so they could figure out what he was telling them.

The lectures were published in a series of small books and sent to groups around the world. One of them profoundly influenced Ernest Holmes in Los Angeles in 1918. Holmes came across the text while visiting a metaphysical library and was inspired to begin a career as a writer and lecturer on metaphysical healing—which he later called the Science of Mind, or Religious Science.

The American historian of religions William James characterized Troward's *Edinburgh Lectures on Mental Science* as "far and away the ablest statement of philosophy I have met, beautiful in its sustained clearness of thought and style; a really classic statement."

Troward went on to write nearly a dozen books and delivered many more lectures (see the list of his works at the back of this book). His writings are still considered the foundation principles of the movement known as New Thought, taught in classes at Unity, Divine Science churches and Centers for Spiritual Living around the world.

On May 16, 1916, at the age of 69, Thomas Troward passed from this plane, absolutely convinced that who and what we are is eternal Spirit, extending Itself in the form of a body for a specific purpose, and operating both in and outside of space and time in an ongoing developmental process that brings each individual to a higher stage of being - and into greater awareness of Oneness with all that is.

SECTION ONE: INTERPRETATION OF ESSAYS

I. A NEW THOUGHT[1]

Thought

These days, people are beginning to realize that thought is a power in itself, one of the great forces of the universe, and ultimately the greatest of forces, directing all the others. This idea seems to be "in the air." It's rapidly spreading through many countries, but it is as yet only vague and nebulous. It's not yet solid, and so isn't yet leading to the practical results that we might expect.

Much evidence has demonstrated that the idea is true: thought *is* the great power of the universe. But to make it practical for our use we must understand the principles by which it works.

We have been like amateurs who want to paint finished pictures before studying the elements of art. When such people see a trained artist do without difficulty what they've tried without success, they see that person as someone special, instead of acknowledging their own lack of knowledge. Like the artist, if we are to get the results we seek, we need to understand that thought is not some indefinable influence floating around and subject to no known laws. We need instead to understand that in fact thought follows laws as uncompromising as those of mathematics, while at the

---

[1] from *The Hidden Power & Other Papers on Mental Science* #4

same time allowing unlimited freedom to the individual.

So, the purpose of the following pages is to suggest a way out of this nebulous sort of thinking into something more solid and reliable.

It's a complex process, and I won't try, in the words of the proverbial country preacher, to "unscrew the inscrutable," for we can never reach a point where there will be nothing inscrutable ahead of us. Still, if I can suggest using a screw-driver instead of a hatchet, and turning the screws from right to left instead of from left to right, it may enable us to loosen some things which would otherwise remain screwed down tight.

We are all learning, and indeed the hopefulness of life is in realizing that there are unending possibilities before us. More, no matter how far we may advance, we'll always be on the edge of something greater. We can be like Peter Pan, the boy who never grew up - heaven defend me from ever feeling quite grown up, for then I should come to a standstill! With that in mind, please take what I have to say simply as the talk of one student to another in the Great School of Life, and don't expect too much.

Existence and Essence

The first question is where to begin. The great philosopher René Descartes began his book with the words *"Cogito, ergo sum."* "I think (or, by another translation, "I am aware"), therefore I am." Let's follow his example.

Two things we can have no doubt about: our own existence and the existence of the world around us. But what in us is aware of these two things? What part of us hopes and fears and plans regarding them? Certainly not our flesh and bones; someone whose leg has been amputated is able to think just the same. It's obvious, therefore, that some part of us receives impressions and forms ideas, then reasons, determines courses of action, and carries them out, which is not the physical body. This is the real "I Myself." This is the person we are really concerned with; and it is bettering this "I Myself" that makes it worth asking what thought has to do with things.

It's equally true, on the other hand, that steam, electricity, gravity, chemical bonds, and the other forces of Nature do not think. They follow certain fixed laws that we humans must accept if we are to function in this world.

Immediately, then, we see two distinct modes of motion — the movement of Thought and the movement of Energy — the first of these being used by the application of consciousness and will, and the second used by the mathematical sequences we call laws.

A symbol for these two modes is the two pillars at the entrance to Solomon's Temple.[2] They are also used in Freemasonry: the pillars are called Jachim and Boaz — the name Jachim coming from the root "Yah" meaning "One," indicating the mathematical element of Law; and the name Boaz from the root "Awáz" meaning "Voice," indicating the personal element of free will. In the Bible and in Freemasonry, the Temple of Truth can only be entered by passing between these two pillars. This tells us that real progress only be can

_____

[2] In the Hebrew Bible (the Christian Old Testament) 1Kings 7:21 and 2Chronicles 3:17

made by accepting that these two modes—mathematical constants and personal will—are the two Pillars of the Universe, and finding the correct balance between them is our life's work.

Taking this logic, the next step, we find that Universal Law and Individual Person are the two great principles with which we have to deal. The problem before us is to clarify their relationship.

Understanding Universal Law

Let's consider some well-established facts in the physical world that demonstrate Universal Law at work under known conditions. This will help us to project how the same Law is likely to work under unknown conditions. We can do this because the Law must be one throughout the universe, even though it appears to work in a variety of ways, because it's applied in so many different ways.

Modern science has shown conclusively that every kind of atom is composed of particles of one original substance which pervades all space, once called the ether, but now known as the quantum field. From this field emerge waves of energy and particles of matter, seemingly at random.

Some of the particles carry a positive charge of electricity and some a negative, and the atom is formed by the grouping of negatively charged particles (electrons) around a center, a nucleus, composed of positive and neutral electrical charges (protons and neutrons). The number of these particles and their motion determine the nature of the atom—whether, for instance, it will be an atom of iron or an atom of hydrogen.

The size of these particles is small indeed, beyond anything but abstract mathematical conception. In fact, scientists have only recently been able to photograph a single atom, which image looks much like a blob of light. Years ago, the British physicist Sir Oliver Lodge is reported to have said, in a lecture delivered at Birmingham, England,

> The chemical atom is as small in comparison to a drop of water as a cricket-ball is compared to the globe of the earth; and yet this atom is as large in comparison to one of its constituent particles as Birmingham town-hall is to a pin's head.

Others have said that in proportion to the size of the particles, the distance at which they revolve around the center of the atom is as great as the distance from the earth to the sun. I leave the realization of such infinite minuteness to the reader's imagination—it's beyond mine.

All material substance, then, that makes up both inanimate matter and our own bodies, proceeds out of the one primary substance that occupies all space in and around us. And out of this homogeneous substance the particles that compose the atom are produced, with positive and negative energy. So now comes the question: what started this shift from the one into two?

Electronic theory does not account for how motion originated; but perhaps another closely allied scientific theory will help us: the study of vibrations and waves. The length of a wave is the distance from the crest of one wave to the crest of the next wave. The illustration on the next page helps us see this:

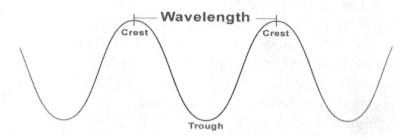

Now modern science recognizes a wide range of waves, from the smallest yet known, 0.1 micron, or about 1/254,000 of an inch, measured by Winfried Schumann in 1893, to waves of many miles in length used in radios (for instance those employed between Clifden in Galway and Glace Bay in Nova Scotia are estimated to have a length of nearly four miles). The first, the infinitesimally small ultra-violet or actinic waves are the essence of photography, and the second, long radio waves carry a signal around the globe and beyond.

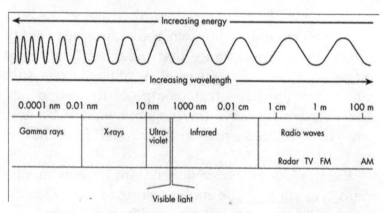

But what starts the vibrations? The German physicist Heinrich Hertz announced his discovery of electromagnetic waves in 1888. He discovered how to

generate these waves by means of sudden, sharply defined, electrical discharges. It's like dropping a stone in
smooth water; the sudden impact sets up a series of
ripples all around the center of the disturbance. The
electrical impulse acts similarly; the fact that the waves
flow in all directions from the central impulse means a
broadcast message may be picked up in any direction
by any receiver tuned to the same rate of vibration.[3]

The eidophone, which was invented, I believe, by
Mrs. Watts-Hughes, is a good example of wave action.
I have seen that lady experiment with it: dry sand is
scattered on a diaphragm on which the vibrations from
music played near it are focused. The sand, as it were,

dances in time to the music, and when the music stops
it's found to settle into definite forms, sometimes like a
tree or flower, or some geometrical figure, but never in
a confused jumble. (Perhaps this is the origin of the

---

[3] AM, FM, and Shortwave are different ways to modulate the waves
and so require different tuners to receive them. Television operates on a
different set of waves and so requires yet another kind of receiver. As do
the cell phone and the wireless internet.

legends regarding the creative power of Orpheus' lyre, and also the sacred dances of the ancients — who knows!?) Today, the science of these patterns is called *cymatics*.

At this point the reader may feel inclined to say, with the old Irishman, that all this is "dry as ditchwater," but it actually has a good deal to do with ourselves, as we shall see.

For now, I want you to realize the fact that the Law can always be trusted. When we see it working under known conditions, we can rely on its unchangingness to infer what it will do under other, hypothetical, or as yet to be discovered, conditions.

And this is precisely the way that many important discoveries have been made. Mendeléef, the Russian chemist, saw a gap in the orderly sequence of the chemical elements, and relying on the old maxim *"Natura nihil facit per saltum"* ("Nature nowhere leaves a gap to jump over") he assumed the existence of three then unknown chemical elements, now called Scandium, Gallium and Germanium. He calculated their atomic weight, chemical affinities, and so on, and when they were discovered many years later, they were found to exactly fit his description. In much the same way, Pierre and Marie Curie discovered radium.

Hertz was led to the discovery of electromagnetic waves in very much the same way. The celebrated mathematician Clerk-Maxwell had calculated all the characteristics of these waves twenty-five years before; then Hertz made his discovery on the basis of those calculations.

In another kind of example, the planet Neptune was discovered by the German astronomer Johan Galle based on calculations made years before by the French astronomer Urbain Le Verrier. The movements of the known planets were mathematically unaccountable except on the hypothesis that some more remote planet existed. Astronomers had faith in the constancy of mathematics and the hypothetical planet was found to be a reality — along with several others, since.

I think these examples will be sufficient to convince the reader that the invariable sequence of Law can be relied upon, that the principles that underlie universal processes are constant, and that by studying those principles under known conditions we may get at least some insight into how they might work under other conditions that haven't yet been observed.

General Law and the Individual

Let's focus now on human beings. Results of experiments in psychical research are finding that our consciousness and capacity to act are not entirely restricted to our physical body. The American poet (and nurse, during the War Between the States), Walt Whitman, was quite right when he said that we are not all "contained between our hat and our boots." So, since all experience, including such non-physical experiences, form part of our environment, they must be included in any exploration of our relation to our universe.

Some very interesting experiments were made at the turn of the 1800s-1900s by the French psychologist Albert de Rochas, which show that under certain conditions the sensation of physical touch can be experienced at some distance from the body. He found that under these conditions the person experimented on doesn't feel the prick of a needle on his skin, but does feels it if the prick is made about an inch-and-a-half away from the surface of the skin. Then, at about three inches from this point the prick of the needle is felt, but not in the space between these two points. Then there's another interval of no sensation, but at about six inches away the subject again feels the sensation, and so on. It appears that the body is surrounded by successive zones of sensation, the first about an inch-and-a-half from the body, and the others at intervals of about three inches each. The number of these zones seems to vary in different cases, but in some there are as many as six or seven, thus giving a radius of sensation that extends more than twenty inches beyond the body.

These results can be understood in terms of what I've already said about waves. The heart and the lungs move rhythmically in the body, and each involves the electrical activity of nerves, creating its own series of electrical vibrations. The vibrations projected by the lungs are estimated to be three times the length of those projected by the heart, while those projected by the heart are three times as rapid as those projected by the lungs. This means that the two sets of waves will sometimes overlap: if the two sets of waves start together the crest of every third wave of the heart's rapid series of short waves will meet the crest of one of the long waves of the lung's slower series, and in between, the short waves will coincide with the depression of one of the long waves.

Now, when the crest of one wave overtakes that of a wave going in the same direction, the two together combine into a single wave of greater height (amplitude) than the original waves would by themselves.

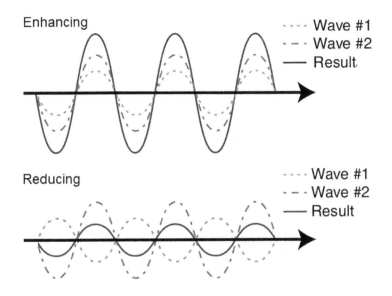

(If the reader has the opportunity to study the waves on the beach you can verify this for yourself—"sneaker waves" being a potentially disastrous example.)

In De Rochas' experiments, it is at these points, when the two waves combine to form a larger wave, that the zones of sensation occur. Then, when the downturn in the larger wave meets the rise in the smaller one, it neutralizes it (again, this is observable at the beach, particularly when the tide is coming in).

Because this double series starts from the interior of the body, the skin, which is several inches from their starting point, may come at one of these neutralized wave-points, so the sensation is neutralized there. This also explains why the succeeding zones of sensation are double the distance from each other.

This is the explanation given by De Rochas, and it provides another example of the principle of mathematical sequence. It would appear that under normal conditions the double series of vibrations is spread all over the body, so all parts are equally sensitive to touch.

The research at the HeartMath Institute supports the work of Rochas in demonstrating that there are waves proceeding from human beings. Work at the Institute of Noetic Sciences (IONS) extends their results to show the physical effect one person's thought may have on another person's physiology, as did the research published by Charles Tart in the 1970s and '80s. Based on this work we have to accept that we humans affect our environments in far more ways than we've generally believed.

The New Thought

Our ancestors had no conception of carriages that could go without horses, yet by a new combination of some elements that have always existed, such vehicles are common in our streets today. Millennia before that, the idea that a cart could be used to carry things could not be imagined. The same process applies to ships, submarines, airplanes, and space vessels—and, of course, the cellphone and computer. Throughout humanity's existence, we can see some form of intelligence making new combinations of the elements that are always present to bring about new results often far beyond our past experiences.

How does this work? Well, it turns out that all advancements of science and engineering have been achieved by a uniform method:

1. asking what the active factor is in something that exists, then
2. asking what makes it go as far as it goes and what prevents it going further, and then,
3. by carefully considering the nature of that factor,
4. finding what sort of conditions allow it to express itself more fully.

This is the scientific method.[4] It has proved itself successful regarding material things and social and organizational processes many times over, and there's no reason why it should not be equally reliable applied to the psycho-spiritual matters we are exploring here.

We ask, then, what the active factor is that operates in the universe as a whole and in ourselves as part of it.

Doing so, we've already seen that there's an invisible power which particularizes the general quantum field into different forms, each with their own mode of motion, from electrical motion in an atom to the simply mechanical motion of the planet, up to the will-directed motion of humans. We accept, therefore, that some one power is the source of *all* motion.

We've also already established that there are two distinct modes of Motion: the Movement of Thought and the Movement of Energy. Therefore, if this invisible power is the source of *all* motion, it must be the source of the capacity to think and feel, as well as to move objects and waves.

---

[4] Most modern teaching of the scientific method focuses on the part of the work described here as "carefully considering the nature:" the formation of an hypothesis, testing it, analyzing the results and publishing the methods used so others may replicate them. But that's only a part of the larger process of scientific inquiry outlined here.

Universal Spirit

We can call this power by any name, but since it is universal (everywhere present) and is motivational (causing motion), the term Universal Spirit can be applied. Our common speech shows how we know this intuitively: we speak of the spirit in which an act is done, of entering into the spirit of a game, of the spirit of the time, and so on. So

> we can say that the primary active factor in the whole universe must be the invisible power of something we shall call Universal Spirit, and it is active in human beings.[5]

Now this invisible power causes all motion leading to the formation of all matter, including planets and the life forms on them, making it the source and essence of Life. And, since the universe is continuing to expand, it's evident that what we're calling Universal Spirit is continually increasing its modes of expression, including livingness. Livingness is clearly, then, not simply material form, but an aspect of the energy governing feeling, thought, and other forms of motion.

A Reversal

What humanity is searching for, then, is not new material forms and conditions, but a way that this livingness, this feeling and thought, may be more completely realized in our lives. Only then can we have the increased substance, in the form of material forms and conditions, that we have sought.

This brings us to the conclusion, therefore, that

---

[5] See Troward's book, *Edinburgh Lectures on Mental Science*. See also texts by quantum physicists, like *Self-Aware Universe* by Amit Goswami and *Quantum Self* by Danah Zohar, for more detailed explanations of how and why this is so.

1. increasing our livingness can occur by bringing the general operation of the Universal Spirit into our personal, individual expression. And

2. this requires that our thoughts and feelings align with the essential movement of the Universal Spirit itself.

This idea, however, is a complete reversal of our old conceptions. Until now we have been told that forms and conditions are the causes of our mental states.[6] Now, however, we are learning that the true order of the creative process is exactly the reverse:

3. thought and feeling are the causes, and forms and conditions are the effects.

This order and this method of thinking are not new. They are older than the foundation of the world, for they are those of the creative Spirit itself; and all through the ages this teaching has been handed down in various forms — the true meaning of which has been perceived by only a few in each generation. But as the light of this understanding breaks in upon any individual it is a new light to that person, and so to each of us it becomes a New Thought.[7]

------

[6] Current medical research has been moving in both directions on this subject: holistic medicine, working with thought and energy are now part of the work of the US National Institutes of Health, while at the same time the relationship between chemicals released by bacteria in the intestines and neuropeptides in the brain are being explored as possible explanations for much of the human condition.

[7] For a history of the application of this way of thinking in the US, see *The Science of Mental Healing* by Ruth L. Miller (Portal Center Press). For an overview of its application in the Tibetan Buddhist tradition, see *Calm Healing* by Robert Bruce Newman and Ruth L. Miller (North Atlantic Books)

New Thought, then, is not the name of a particular sect, but is rather the essential factor for our individual development. Everyone who finds this new basis of thinking experiences the cosmos in a radically different way, for from this standpoint each of us is not just a part of the general effect, but part of the cause.

Having learned this lesson, we now have the foundation for applying the universal law of the creative process in our individual lives.

The New Understanding

Having seen and felt this new understanding, each person then understands that they can only experience more power and wisdom by letting the general cause we're calling Universal Spirit flow more and more freely into their own center of awareness. This realization then leads the individual to find ways to develop the conditions that allow this to happen.

Here, again, the scientific method can be used.

First the observation: we can see that this universal causative power is always expanding and adapting. We see it in the mechanism of the planets, in the production of supply to support physical life, and in the maintenance of humanity as a whole. It is always learning and adjusting. Because these are the activities of intelligence, we must call this power a form of intelligence.

As this intelligence explores and develops, it follows an orderly sequence of growth, which we call evolution. There are many individual failures along the way, but there is no cosmic failure, and any apparent individual failure contributes information to the cosmic developmental process.

Observing this cosmic process in our own lives, we can see that individual failures diminish in proportion to our recognition of the Universal Spirit at work. Haven't we all had terrible failures that turned out to be huge blessings?

As our minds are centered on its activity the Universal Spirit can take a new starting point within our minds and bodies, allowing for a new level of development. More, this principle that we have called Universal Spirit in no way changes its essential nature when working through our being – the same way that electricity losing none of its essential qualities when passing through wires to manifest as light.

As we understand all these principles and processes, our new line of thinking runs something like the following:

My mind is a center of intelligence, an expression of the underlying force, the Universal Spirit, which forms and motivates all things.

Universal Spirit is constantly expanding into fuller expression, and so is always producing something beyond what has gone before: something entirely new, not included in past experience, though proceeding out of it by an orderly sequence of growth.

Since Spirit cannot change its inherent nature, it must operate in the same manner in me as it does everywhere around me.

Therefore, in my own special world, of which I am the center, Spirit is always moving to produce new conditions, always advancing beyond any that have gone before.

This is a legitimate line of argument from the premises established so far. The intelligence and motion that we have called Universal Spirit determines the forms that manifest in the universe and in our own particular world, as well as supplying the energy for their production. It is forming everything throughout nature, so if we are to apply it in our personal world, we must learn to trust that it is doing so.

The Creative Process

But then the question naturally arises, "If this is how it works, what part does the individual play?" When we remember that our thoughts go out into the world as waves, the answer becomes clear:

> our thoughts and feelings, focusing in a specific direction, aligning with the creative process of Universal Spirit, channel Spirit's process into the particular forms of our thoughts.

That is, to participate in the creative process, we choose to become a center of its action by

1. aligning our own individual thought and feeling with that of Universal Spirit, then
2. allowing Spirit to bring about our intended form in the world around us.

Universal Spirit acts through forces which attract and repel, as in positive and negative charges, and in the poles of a magnet. As an expression of that Spirit, therefore, each individual generates a force of attraction in accordance with the pattern of their particular individuality. When we express our hopes, fears, or expectations, the result is that we intensify the universal forces in a specific way and they then begin to act both through us and around us along the lines of our expression. In short,

> we draw to ourselves those people, events, and objects that fit our way of being.

This principle can be called the Law of Attraction.

Aligning with Spirit

As we align our thoughts and feelings with the Law of Spirit, we are pulled into that way of being, drawing to us what we are focusing on, and, at the same time, being drawn into wherever we focus. Thus, we are attracted towards the Universal Spirit. This attraction follows the lines of least resistance, the lines most natural to our own unique bent of mind.

We can say, then, that this Law of Attraction is the reciprocal action between the intelligence of Universal Spirit and the individual mind. When our desires are directed to reproducing the Universal Spirit's activity, they are bound to externalize in our world as things and circumstances corresponding to our unique form of being and so enhance our lives.[8]

Completing the Creative Process

That does not complete the process, however. Once these external factors appear in our life, we must work on them as objects and conditions that we can affect.

This is where many people fall short of completing the work they hope to accomplish. They realize and work with the inner, subjective, or creative process, but don't see that it must be followed by an outer, objective, or constructive process, and consequently they

---

[8] This is the meaning of the New Testament injunction: "seek ye first the kingdom of heaven and all things follow" (Matthew 6:33)

become impractical dreamers and never reach the final stage of a completed work.

> The creative process brings the materials and conditions for the work to our hands; then we must make use of them with diligence and common-sense.

As the old saying goes, "God will provide the food, but He will not cook the dinner."

This, then, is the part taken by the individual, and this is how individuals become a distributing center of the Universal energy. We are neither trying to lead it like a blind force nor are we under a blind, unreasoning compulsion from it.

No Sacrifice, Just Following Consistent Laws

When we receive material support it's because we seek material resources. When we receive guidance it's because we seek guidance. We seek and receive both according to a Law that we now recognize.

In physical science nature obeys us precisely to the same extent that we first obey nature. An engineer submits to the laws of electricity in order to apply them to some specific purpose, and spiritual science works in the same way. We no more sacrifice our freedom or reduce our personal power in this process than does the engineer working with electricity. In fact, the more intimate our knowledge of this science becomes, the more we find that it leads to true Liberty.

The key is the new thought: it *must* create new conditions because it operates within the true order of the creative process.

As the esoteric maxim of ancient occult science has it, "What is a truth on one plane is a truth on all."

Therefore, if we would bring a new level of Life, Light, and Liberty into our lives, we must bring a new understanding of those ideas into our thought. We must find in ourselves the starting point of a new creative series, not by the force of personal will, but by union with the Universal Spirit. We must become the expression of its inherent Love and Beauty that makes all things new.

ESSENTIAL POINTS

- In many fields of science, thought is beginning to be understood to have power. To understand how this may be so, consider the following line of reasoning:
  1. The universe is filled with one common substance, the quantum field;
  2. Every form of matter and energy arises from this quantum field, through the interaction of attracting and repelling forces;
  3. The process that causes the differentiation of this uniform field into these different forces, leading to the many different forms of matter and energy is the cause and basis for everything that exists, from stars and planets to the individual person, plant, or animal;
  4. It is also the cause of all movement in physical objects and in living beings, including thought and feeling.
  5. This process has no physical form; it causes these things, not by physical action, but through an expression of its essence.
  6. We may call this process by any name, but because it is universal (everywhere present) and motivational (causes movement and change), we shall call it Universal Spirit.

7. The expression of Universal Spirit is the fundamental cause of all existence and movement in our universe, including all forms of being and Life itself.

8. Universal Spirit is constantly expanding through the interaction of attracting and repelling forces, so we draw to ourselves those people, events, and objects that fit our way of being, repelling those which don't.

•   This understanding is the New Thought that reverses our old idea that matter is the source and cause of all experience and replaces it with the realization that the expression of Universal Spirit is the only cause, and all forms of matter and energy are the effect.

•   An individual's experiences are therefore the results of their thoughts and feelings, and aligning their thoughts and feelings with the essence we call Universal Spirit leads to new, more fulfilling and satisfying conditions.

•   Our desires and creative effort should not be directed to material forms and conditions so much as to reproducing in ourselves Spirit's activity in order to externalize the things and circumstances that enhance our lives.

•   This internal, subjective, creative process must be followed by an external, objective, constructive process on the emerging forms for the work to be completed.

Exercises

1. Remember a time when you had a desire that, to all appearances should not come true but did. How were you feeling at that time? What were you thinking?

    a. Notice that the mental state associated with these events is not one of concentration on the desired object but is almost unrelated to the desire.

    b. Notice that the emotional state is joyful and playful, in alignment with Universal Spirit, rather than earnest.

2. Consider a time when you won a prize - or someone you know did - that was exactly what you (or they) wanted. How were you (they) feeling at that time? What were you (they) thinking?

    a. Notice that the mental state associated with these events is not one of concentration on the desired object but is almost unrelated to the desire.

    b. Notice that the emotional state is joyful and playful, in alignment with Universal Spirit, rather than earnest.

3. Consider a time when you thought you (or God, or your boss or spouse) had failed miserably. How were you (they) feeling at that time? What were you (they) thinking?

    a. Notice what happened in the resolution of that event. What kind of thoughts were you thinking? Did you reach a point of "giving up" or "surrender"?

    b. Now consider your current life. How did that apparent failure contribute to your current situation? What have been the blessings emerging from it?

II. A SCIENCE OF SPIRIT[9]

Life and Spirit

Universal Spirit is a center from which growth takes place by expansion in every direction. It pervades all things and is at the heart of all appearances. It is the principle at the root of all that exists – and so we may also call it Life.

This is not the life we see in particular forms; it's something more interior and concentrated than that. It is, instead, a unity that has not yet expanded into diversity, not yet differentiated into any specific mode or form. Life is the sum-total of all its undistributed powers; none of them in particular, but all of them in potential.

This undifferentiated, universal life-power is pure essence, pure energy, pure being. It is that which knows itself and recognizes itself, but which cannot dissect itself because it is not built up of parts, but is ultimately integral. It's one complete unit, responding as a whole to all inputs. In physics, we might call this essence of Life a *holon*[10], or a Bose-Einstein condensate, or a super-conductor. It is pure unity.

Life in its essence is truly unknowable, not un-thinkable but rather un-analyzable. It can't be the

---

[9] from *The Hidden Power & Other Papers on Mental Science* #4

[10] The term is from the Greek, meaning a complete unit. Some say the human mind is a holon because it tends to function this way.

subject of knowledge, because knowledge estimates distinctions and *relationships* between things. We can say "we know" only when we see things in relation to others. Here, though, we are beyond any question of relations; we are face-to-face with absolute Oneness.

Analyzing Spirit

The value of analysis is that it leads us to the original starting-point of whatever we're analyzing and so teaches us the laws by which its final form emerges. The botanist, for example, analyses a flower by pulling it to pieces, then builds up from those carefully studied fragments a synthesis of Nature's construction process, and so discovers the laws of the formation of all flower-forms. So, like a botanist who has discovered the law of the flower's construction, we can apply the law that we've discovered in one form to other forms and so turn our analysis into a synthesis.

Most modern scientists, materialistic as they've been trained to be, never treat the un-analyzable essence in this way when they experience it in the laboratory. They state that what is unexplainable is simply energy of some kind, probably heat or motion. They do so because they realize that the conservation of energy, its indestructibility, and the impossibility of adding to or detracting from the sum-total of energy in the world, is the one unchanging fact on which the all materialist science is based. All their materialistic knowledge draws from this knowledge of "the unknowable." Yet, when pressed to explain this particular "unknowable" that we've called Universal Spirit they have no answers. And so this power is always beyond the reach of traditional science. It cannot be used or understood by those who consider "the unknowable" to be the same as "not-existing."

We, however, apply our understanding of the law of Life, the unity of Universal Spirit, and so we find the root of all other knowledge, and come into the secret of all power, as have thousands of wise people around the world over the millennia. Having realized that this universal and unlimited energy or power that we are calling Spirit is the root of all things and also of ourselves, we have obtained the key to the whole; we shall nowhere find anything else but individual variations on this one universal principle.

The Spiritual Side of Science

The science of Spirit is no less scientific than the science of matter; it starts from the same fact:

> there is, everywhere, an intelligent energy which defies definition or explanation.

And it goes on from there through the same orderly process of observation and testing.

Spiritual Science differs from the science of matter, however, in that it goes beyond simply observing and naming the unknowable, that indestructible energy that underlies everything, to contemplate and study it as an aspect of responsive intelligence.

Although this idea does not yet fall within the scope of current, materialist, physical science, (outside of certain theoreticians in quantum mechanics and intelligent design), the science of Spirit and the science of matter are not opposed. They are complementary; neither is fully comprehensible without some knowledge of both. Further, since they are simply two aspects of one whole, they shade into each other so gently that no arbitrary line can be drawn between them.

Limitations of Materialism

Science studied in a truly scientific spirit, following out its own deductions unflinchingly to their legitimate conclusions, will always reveal the twofold aspect of things, the inner and the outer, and it is only a truncated and maimed science that refuses to recognize both. As the famous physicist Albert Einstein is often quoted as saying, "Science without religion is blind; religion without science is lame."

Therefore, the legitimate study of the material world is not Materialism. Materialism is that limited view of the universe which only allows the existence of mechanical effects from mechanical causes.

> A system that recognizes no higher power than the physical forces of nature must logically result in having no explanation for its observations except some as-yet undiscovered physical force or some fraud.

And history shows us that the logical results of such explanations are perfidy and violence. So, since we wish to avoid encouraging the mode of thought that led to the distresses in the Italy of the Borgias, in the France of the First Revolution, and in the Union of Soviet Socialist Republics, we shall set ourselves, instead, to study that aspect of things whose logical results are in alignment with truth and love.

The Cube as a Model

The cube is the shape of perfect stability which can never be overthrown. Whatever side you turn it on, it remains the perfect cube, always standing upright; you

cannot upset it. It represents the manifestation in concrete solidity of that central, life-giving energy which is
not located on any one plane but generates all the
planes: the above, the below, and all four sides. This is
why, in the Christian New Testament book of Revela-
tion, the apostle John describes the heavenly Jerusalem
(a word that means "place of peace") as a cube; "the
length and the breadth and the height of it are equal."

At the same time John's New Jerusalem is a city, a
place of habitation, where Universal Spirit (by whatever name we call it) has its dwelling. We know this is
accurate because in our analysis we have seen that Life,
as Universal Spirit, must dwell everywhere.

And, just as one plane of a cube tells us the nature
of all the other planes and also whatever is within the
cube, so any plane of manifestation in this universe
implies the others and also that which is "within". It's
only when we argue about things from without, instead of from within, that our true perception of their
nature is lost. Hence the New Testament tells us, "The
Kingdom of Heaven is within you."

So, to make any progress in the spiritual side of
science — and *every* field of science has its spiritual side
— we must always keep our minds fixed on this "innermost within" that we have called Universal Spirit,
as the dimension that generates the outer manifestation
being studied.

ESSENTIAL POINTS

- Life is the center which expands in every direction; it
  pervades all things and is at the heart of all appearances; it is absolute, universal, and we call it Universal
  Spirit.

- This is "the unknowable," not in the sense of the un-thinkable but of the un-analyzable; we can't analyze it but we can see its expression as our world; yet it cannot be used or understood by those who consider "the unknowable" to be the same as "not-existing."

- The science of Spirit is distinguished from the science of matter in that it goes beyond simply naming the indestructible "unknowable" energy that underlies everything, contemplating and studying it.

- When we apply our understanding of the law of unity of Universal Spirit we access the same power as wise people of all ages.

- Just as one plane of a cube tells us the nature of all the other planes and also whatever is within it, so any plane of manifestation in this universe implies all the others and also the Spirit within that generates them.

- The science of Spirit and the science of matter are simply two aspects of one whole: outer and inner, and the science of Spirit focuses on the inner.

Exercises

1. Observe two leaves: one living and green on its plant; the other dead and separated from the plant.
    a. What are some of the differences?
    b. The similarities?
2. Compare the living leaf to an animal, to your own body.
    a. What are some of the differences?
    b. The similarities?
3. Imagine, draw, or pick up a cube. Look at how the sides are exactly the same measurements and shape. Notice how it sits stable on a flat surface, with no tendency to wobble or turn. Think about what the shape and forces are in the center of the cube, holding it together.
    a. How is your body, your life, like this cube?
    b. How is the universe, this planet, like this cube?

III. POWER AND PERSONALITY[11]

The Intelligence and Responsiveness of Spirit

No one can deny that there is an intelligent order present throughout the natural cosmos. The more deeply we investigate the world we live in, the more we see that all our science is the translation into words or numerical symbols of an order that already exists. There is no random work here. Every attraction and repulsion acts with its proper force collecting the atoms into molecules, the molecules into tissues, the tissues into organs, the organs into individuals, and the individuals into organizations.

Clearly, the emergence of all things is guided by some unfailing intelligence that harmonizes the entire universe in all the wonderful ways that materialist science describes more clearly every day. Indeed, it may be said that if a clear statement of this existing order is the highest level of intelligence that the human intellect can reach, there must be a correspondingly greater in-

---

[11] from *The Hidden Power & Other Papers on Mental Science* #4

ɔlligence that gives rise to such great order and inter-related complexity!

For example, observe how, at each stage of the development process we get the sum of the intelligent forces that operate in the constituent parts, *plus* a higher degree of intelligence, something that belongs to the system *as a whole,* and not just the parts. This is a radical law which we cannot consider too deeply:

> the degree of intelligence at work is a function of the complex wholeness of the organism.

This means that the more highly organized systems have a greater degree of intelligence and so are able to affect (and even direct) all lower or less fully-integrated systems of being.

Now, unless we hypothesize a workman working upon material external to himself—in which case we have to explain the existence of the workman—this intelligence must be an aspect of the Universal Spirit that is everywhere, at the heart of all appearances, because there is no other source from which it could proceed. Therefore, we may describe Universal Spirit as universal Intelligence.

The Personal in the Universal

Being intelligent, the Universal Spirit *knows,* and what it knows is Itself. Spirit being ultimately present in and throughout all there is, Spirit knows its Self at all Its levels of being, from the innermost component of the atom through the minerals and plants and animals and humans to the most complex galactic systems and beyond. The higher levels of system recognize the lower levels, and accordingly, the lower levels recognize the higher.

This being so, we can begin to see that Spirit, as the "innermost within" of all things, under whatever exterior manifestation It is revealed can be expected to be responsive as well as intelligent. Knowing Its Self, and recognizing Its Self at all levels, and seeking constantly to expand Its expression at all levels, Spirit must be responsive to *any* activity at *any* level.

The combination of intelligence and responsiveness implies the presence of personality. Thus, we may therefore now explore the possibility that the Universal Spirit contains elements of personality. Let's consider this idea.

Human beings have a sense of person as well as the unique qualities of an individual that we call personality. Then, on the principle that you cannot get something out of a bag that doesn't contain any of that thing, we may say that our own personality must have its origin in something with personality. That is, if we have personality, whatever composes and sustains us must have personality. By this logic we can see that, since we are personal in our nature, Universal Spirit must be personal in its nature.

Now human personality is not simply an assemblage of parts, whether spiritual or material, but is the synthesis of those parts into one unified whole. More, as we discovered is the case with Life in its essence, the human personality is a *holon*, in which there is no separation of the parts; any action on any part of a person affects the whole, instantaneously.

This unity is superior, both in intelligence and power, to any less fully integrated mode of Spirit – as, for example, a swarm of bees, a forest, or a rock.

Also, in humanity we find personality realized more clearly than in other kingdoms of nature. We can even say that in humanity the synthesis of Spirit's personal nature has proceeded far enough that we can recognize ourselves as individual expressions of that personality.

Finally, using the intelligence of Universal Spirit that is expanding into and as each being, and following this line of reasoning, we begin see that we humans are Spirit and therefore all that is true of Spirit must also be true of each of us, at some level of our being.

Limits on the Power of Thought

Now we've seen that Spirit is bound to respond to itself in all degrees and at all levels. This means that, even in those forms of being in which Spirit is not sufficiently synthesized to render a particular personality, Spirit is nonetheless present and recognizes Its Self. This fact, that Spirit recognizes Itself in all material forms, is what allows human thought to externalize itself in all the infinite forms we choose.

That is, however, provided that we honor another equally fundamental law that restrains our abuse of that power. That other law is that

> we can command the universal powers for our own purposes only insofar as we first realize and obey their generic character.

In the material world this means, for example, that humanity can employ water for any purpose which does not require it to run up-hill, and can use electricity for any purpose that does not require it to pass from a lower to a higher potential. Universal Spirit also has a generic character with which we must comply if we are to employ it for our specific purposes.

Universal Spirit is Life; hence Its fundamental tendency must always be to increase the aliveness of every individual. And since It is universal, Its action must always be equally for the benefit of all. Thus

the generic character of Spirit is to act for the benefit of all.

And just as water or electricity, or any other of the physical forces of the universe, will not work contrary to their generic character, so Spirit will not work contrary to Its generic character, which, for lack of a better term, we will call "goodness."

The inference is obvious. If we would use the power of Universal Spirit we must follow the law of the Spirit, which is what we are calling "goodness." This is the only limitation:

if our originating intention is good, we may employ the spiritual power for whatever purpose we will.

And how is "goodness" to be defined? For the Universal Spirit, it means to the benefit of all - enhancing our own individual wellbeing and that of all beings, equally.

ESSENTIAL POINTS
- An unfailing intelligence harmonizes the entire universe in all the wonderful ways that materialist science describes.

- If we hypothesize a workman to explain this intelligence, we have to explain the existence of the workman; therefore, this intelligence must be in the Universal Spirit that we have discovered is everywhere, at the heart of all appearances.
- Intelligence controls each organism and is a function of the complex wholeness of an organism.
- Higher-level systems are able to exercise control over lower or less fully-integrated systems, and Spirit is the highest level system of being.
- Human thought, as a more fully integrated expression of Spirit, may express itself in limitless forms among less organized systems of being.
- We can command natural powers for our own purposes only insofar as we realize and obey their generic character (For example, we can use water for any purpose that does not require it to run up-hill.).
- Universal Spirit is Life, always increasing the aliveness of every individual, and its action must always be equally for the benefit of all.
- If our intention is for the benefit of all, we may employ the spiritual power for whatever purpose we will.

Exercises
1. Recognizing that Spirit is present in all things and that, since Spirit has personality all beings must have personality,
    a. consider a pet that you know—your own or someone else's that you've been able to observe closely. What kinds of personality traits have you observed?
    b. Now consider a fly or other insect that you've observed for a few minutes. Can you detect the personality there?

     c. Read J. Allen Boone's book *Kinship with All Life* to experience some remarkable examples of the personality in various animals and insects.

2. Recognizing that Spirit is present in all things and that, since we have personality, Spirit must have personality, take an hour or so in a quiet space—preferably in nature, but in a room will do—somewhere you can relax completely, and focus your attention on a rock.

     a. Using all your senses, allow yourself to be aware of the nature of the rock.

     b. See if you can't discover what the rock is aware of and what it may have to say to you.

3. Recognizing that Spirit is present in all things and that Its fundamental activity is enhancing Life for the benefit of all, think about your current intentions and desires.

     a. To what extent do they conform with the nature and power of Spirit?

     b. How might you modify them to be empowered by Spirit?

     c. Make a list of desires/intentions for your next day, month, year, and life that would benefit yourself and all beings. Fold it up and put it somewhere you will only find every now and then, so you can see how your life reflects this list—how Spirit, through attracting and repelling, has manifested its Self as your desires.

     d. For a month, spend some time as nearly every day as you can, simply contemplating the Universal Spirit in all Its aspects and qualities.

     e. On a special day each season, or each year, go back and review the list you have tucked away. Make a new one, if needed to reflect where you are in your experience, thoughts, and feelings now.

IV. APPLYING THE PRINCIPLES[12]

Applying any principle involves two factors:

- the principle itself, which is the active factor, and
- the subject-matter on which it acts, the passive factor.

While the principle is invariable in all applications, the matter on which it is working is variable. This means that one principle operating on different variables will produce different results. To state this principle mathematically, the variables a, b or c multiplied by the factor x give the results ax, bx, and cx, which differ from one another, even though the factor x remains the same.

So we must not allow ourselves to be misled by appearances.

---

[12] from *The Hidden Power & Other Papers on Mental Science* #4

Continuity of Principle

If a principle exists at all, it exists universally: above and below, within and without. This means it must apply to our spiritual nature as well as the material world. This is the doctrine of continuity:

> each fundamental law applies on the spiritual as well as on the physical plane, and acts with the same mathematical precision on both.

It's the basis for the old-world saying that "a truth on one plane is a truth on all."

We have seen that there are two forms of energy: Thought and Motion. We have also seen that they have power to affect matter only to the extent that they are in harmony with the primary active factor in the universe, an intelligence that benefits all equally, which we have called Universal Spirit. More, we have seen that Spirit is increasingly integrated in life forms until, in humanity, individuals can recognize themselves as the expressions of Universal Spirit in their individuality.

A single principle, common alike to material and spiritual law, therefore, fully accounts for all claims that have ever been made for the creative power of human thought. It also explains humanity's ability to use and manage, our "dominion over," all things that come within the circle of our own particular life. Indeed, it is the reason that

> we have the power, by directing our own thought, to control everything in the world we experience.

Centers within Centers

Each of us is truly the center of our own universe, which extends out infinitely in all directions from our bodies. As such we are constantly creating and developing the world around us, through the two forms of energy: Thought and Motion.

At the same time, each of us is part of a higher system in which we are only one of innumerable similar elements, and this system is part of a higher system, which is part of a still higher system, ongoing until we reach the supreme center of all things. Just as an atomic particle is part of an atom is part of a molecule is part of an organ is part of an organism is part of a social organization is part of an ecosystem is part of a planet and so on... we are part of ever-increasing systems of complexity.

Intelligence and power increase throughout this system of systems, from center to center, in an exponentially increasing ratio, rising with amazing rapidity, until they culminate in the unlimited intelligence and power of All-Being, which we have called the Universal Spirit.

We have seen that humanity uses intention and command to relate to the material forms that are less integrated modes of Spirit, but what is our relation to these higher modes of being? To answer this question, we need to understand the relationship between wholes and parts.

In our bodies, or any other harmoniously structured system, the whole never interferes with the free operation of its parts in the performance of their functions.[13] The lung cell functions freely and adapts with the body's changing activity level, and all is well. The individual applies creativity and effort to accomplish the organization's mission, and both benefit from the result. It is precisely by means of this ongoing relation that each part is maintained in a position to accomplish all the functions for which it is fitted.

This means that the movement of the whole necessarily carries the part along with it. Then, so long as the part allows itself to be carried onward, it is free to work in any direction that fits its own individuality.

And, since the collective individuality of humanity is only a larger scale of the personal individuality, whatever action truly develops the inherent powers of the individual must therefore necessarily be in line with evolution of humanity as a whole.

Further, to maintain our healthy action within the circle of our own individual world we must continually move with the movement of the larger whole. [14]

Relating to the One Mind

Now the same responsiveness of Spirit which we experience as obedience to our wishes when we look to

---

[13] This idea applies to organizations as well as bodies and ecosystems: a good manager lets the worker do the job without interference as long as the job is getting done in a way that contributes to the function of the whole.

[14] This truth was set forth in the ancient Hindu religion as the Car (carriage) of Jagannath. "Jagannath" means "Lord of the Universe," and thus signifies the Universal Mind. This, by the law of Being, must always move forward regardless of any attempts of individuals to restrain it. Those who mount upon its car move onward with it to endlessly advancing evolution, while those who seek to oppose it must be crushed beneath its wheels, for it is no respecter of persons as it unceasingly moves forward—hence later ages degraded the idea into a "juggernaut."

forms with lesser degrees of synthesis of Spirit than our own must also manifest itself when we look to the Spirit of which we are a part. This must be so because of the principle of Continuity we just explored, and because, as we discovered with the interior of the cube, we are looking at higher degrees of *our own internal self.*

If we would use the universal law of Spirit to manage our own individual worlds, then, we must also recognize the supreme center round which we ourselves revolve.

This is not, however, done in the old way we may have been taught. We are not supposing that this center is some being external to ourselves that can be persuaded or cajoled into giving us the good which we are not good enough to give ourselves. No. So long as we retain that infantile idea we have not come into the liberty that results from knowledge of the certainty of universal Law.

Only our ignorance of our relation to the whole makes it appear that we have separate interests. Recognizing the principle of Continuity, we can accept that

> the whole can have no interest contrary to the interest of parts of which it is composed, and no part can have an interest adverse to the whole.

So we need not fear that supreme Intelligence with the old fear which came from ignorance. Supreme Intelligence must be Supreme Law, and the result of studying, understanding, and obeying this Supreme Law is that we acquire the power to use it. It can be counted upon with the same accuracy and dependability as any of the laws of the physical world, but in a much larger domain.

Making our individual thoughts subject to the laws of the One Mind of Universal Spirit is, therefore, far from giving up our liberty; it's the very condition which makes liberty — even life itself — possible. Recognizing that we are alive and have power in our world because we are part of something that functions in a certain way gives us the freedom to use that power in the way that bests suits our own well-being.

All for One and One for All

We are part of what we once feared, and the well-being of the whole depends on the well-being of the part, and vice versa. More, the increased life and vitality of the parts means the increased vitality of the whole.

And since Spirit can only be understood as the continually expanding principle of Life, the demand for any increase in liveliness must, by the inherent nature of the Universal Spirit, be met by a corresponding supply of continually growing intelligence and power. Thus, by a natural law of growth, the supply constantly increases, and this supply may be freely applied to any and every subject that enters our awareness.

It is possible to lose sight of our place in relation to the whole, to take such a narrow view of our own nature (a limited self-centeredness) that doesn't realize that our very life is drawn from this relation with the Universal. Such thinking leads to ignorance of our own possibilities and consequently the limitation of our powers.

In truth, however, as all our exploration so far has demonstrated,

there is no limit to the supply of this energy—
other than what we ourselves put on it by our
thought.

Nor is there any limit to the purposes we may make it
serve, other than the one grand law of Order, by which
good things used for wrong purposes (i.e., other than
for the benefit of all) cause harm to the user. Our understanding of the intelligent and responsive nature of
the Universal Spirit shows that there can be no limitations but these. The one is a limitation inherent in Spirit
itself, and the other is a limitation rooted in our own
ignorance.

The Law of Spirit at All Levels

The Law of Spirit, to which our investigation has
now led us, is infinite in its scope. We have followed it
from the conception of the intelligence of Spirit as observed in the initial atoms to the synthesis of this
intelligence into the conscious identity of the individual human being. But there is no reason why this law
should cease to operate at this point, or at any point
short of the whole.

The test of the soundness of any principle is that
it can operate as effectively on a large scale as on
a small one.

Though the nature of its effect is determined by the nature of the principle itself, the extent of its field is
unlimited.

If, therefore, we continue to follow our inquiry into
the law we have been considering, it leads us to an intelligence as far superior to that of the individual
person as an individual's intelligence is superior to that
of the intelligence of any atom in the body. And, be-

cause of this principle, we understand the collective individuality and spiritual character of any group of human beings: the inhabitants of a city, a district, a country, or of the entire world. Indeed, the American philosopher Ralph Waldo Emerson spoke of "one mind common to all humanity" in his essay "History."

On the same principle there would be a superior collective individuality for the entire solar system, and finally we reach the supreme intelligence of Universal Spirit bringing together in its Self the collective individualities of all the systems in the universe.

This is by no means a merely fanciful notion. It is the law by which our own conscious individuality is constituted, and we find the analogous principle working universally on the physical plane.[15]

We have discovered our individual selves to be a necessary and integral part of the infinite harmony of all-being. We're not merely recognizing this great truth as a vague intuition, but as the logical and unavoidable result of the existence of a universal life-principle which permeates all Nature. Intuition and investigation agree then, on our unique, individual place in the great scheme of things.

A Working Power

Yet even the most advanced among us have, as yet, little more than the faintest notion of what this place is.

---

[15] It is known in materialist science as the "law of inverse squares." The forces of reciprocal attraction or repulsion, as the case may be, are not merely equal to the sum of the forces emitted by the two bodies, but are these two forces multiplied together and divided by the square of the distance between them, so that the resultant power continually rises in a rapidly-increasing ratio as the two bodies approach one another.

It is the place of *power*.

Turning our focus toward those higher modes of spirit which we speak of as "the Universal," the law of Continuity and Flow tells us that

> when we focus on the Universal Spirit, humanity's inmost nature draws into our individual essence an inexhaustible supply of light and power.

> And, when we focus on the forms holding lesser degrees of Spirit's manifestation that fill each person's particular world, the individual becomes the center of energy and order for that world.

Can we imagine any position in the universe containing greater possibilities than these?

Ralph Waldo Emerson, who thought of himself as a poet, has rightly said that a little algebra will often do far more towards clearing our ideas than a large amount of poetic simile. In algebra, comparing various powers of x with that same x multiplied by infinity eliminates any difference between them: $3x\infty=\infty$; $5,6767x\infty=\infty$; $15,482,335x\infty=\infty$; etc. This is because there can be no ratio between any number and the infinite; they are now the same value. In the same way the relation between the individual and the infinite Spirit must always remain the same, regardless of whatever power or wealth is attained by the individual.[16]

But this in no way interferes with the Law of Growth, by which the individual rises to higher and

---

[16] I trust unmathematical readers will pardon my using this method of statement for the benefit of others to whom it will carry conviction. A relation once clearly grasped in its mathematical aspect becomes thenceforth one of the unalterable truths of the universe, no longer a thing to be argued about, but an axiom which may be assumed as the foundation on which to build up the edifice of further knowledge.

higher levels, and therefore powers, of his own individuality.

Because we are what we are, we all may become
what we will.

The Word

Students of the Jewish mystical path called *Kabbal*
tell us of "the lost word," the word of power which
humanity has lost. They say that, to the person who
discovers this word all things are possible.

Is this miracle-working word really lost? Yes and
No. It is the open secret of the universe, and the New
Testament gives us the key to it. It tells us, "The Word
is nigh thee, even in thy mouth and in thy heart."[17]

It is the most familiar of all words, the word which
in our heart we realize as the center of our conscious
being, and which is in our mouth a hundred times a
day. It's the word "I AM." It tells us

> "My particular individuality is one of the ways
> the Infinite expresses itself, and therefore I am,
> in and of myself, the very power that we have
> found to be the innermost within of all things.
> Because I am what I am, I may be what I will to
> be."

It serves us to pay heed to the great teachers of the ages
who have taught that all power is in the "I AM," and to
accept this teaching by our faith in their authority.

That's much better than not accepting it at all, but
the more excellent way is to understand why they
taught such a thing, and to realize for ourselves this
first great law.

---

[17] Christian New Testament, Romans 10:8.

We have lost, not the word, but the realization of its power. And as the infinite depths of meaning which the words I AM carry with them open out to us, we begin to realize the stupendous truth that

we ourselves are the very power which we seek.

Polarity as a Continuum of Power

Now the forms of everything in the natural world depend on the simple law by which there can be no inside without an outside, no magnetic pole without a corresponding opposite pole, nor one end of a stick without an opposite end. This we shall call the Law of Polarity. To understand this more fully, consider:

- life is motion, and
- all motion is energy appearing at some point other than its origin, and,
- when any work has been done, appearing in another form than at its origin.
- It's still the same energy, wherever, and in whatever new form it reappears.

In materialist science this is the doctrine of the conservation of energy. Because of this law, the smallest flame has all the qualities of a bonfire.

It is a demonstration of the principle of Continuity we explored earlier: the continuum from the universal to the particular carries with it all its inherent powers. This means the I AM in the individual can be none other than the I AM in the universal working in the smaller sphere that is each of us. It is the same power.

This is the great truth which the ancients set forth as the "Macrocosm in the Microcosm": the lesser I AM reproduces the precise image of the greater. It is also the truth which the Hebrew Bible tells us when it speaks of humanity as the image of God. [Genesis 1:26]

Now the immense practical importance of this principle is that it is the key to the great law that "as a man thinks so he is."[18] The explanation may be stated as follows:

1. We know by personal experience that we experience life in two ways:
   a. our power to act and
   b. our ability to feel, to be susceptible to sensation and emotion.

2. The individual and the universal are two ends of a continuum.

3. Spirit therefore acts and is sensitive, and being infinite must be infinitely sensitive to the slightest touch — every thought, feeling, word, or action — anywhere and everywhere;

4. As our thought conforms to and sends its vibrating currents into the infinity of Spirit, it then produces currents of like quality but of far vaster power — just as the bonfire has more power than the flame of a candle.

5. As Spirit is the creative power of the universe, the impact of our thought upon it thus sets in motion a creative force.

6. Thoughts persistently conforming to Spirit's nature will naturally produce a greater external effect than casual ones not centered upon any particular object.

---

[18] Taken from the Hebrew Bible (Proverbs 23:7) this phrase was also used by James Allen in 1912 as the title of his most famous book, which is interpreted in the Library of Hidden Knowledge series in *As We Think So We Are.*

7. Scattered thoughts which recognize no principle of unity will fail to produce any principle of unity; similarly

   a. The thought that we are weak and have no power over circumstances results in inability to control circumstances, and

   b. any thought of our power in the world produces the experience of that power.

8. As this law holds good for one thought it holds good for all our thinking;

9. Hence, we are continually creating for ourselves a world which accurately reproduces our own thoughts.

This power of our thought is inherent in us because of our essential spiritual nature, and we cannot rid ourselves of it.

We constantly make our thoughts manifest in our lives and world.

More, the power of our thought is a power which, if it is not used to enhance life, will be destructive—as the Hindus recognize in their god Shiva, whom they call "the Destroyer." If not intelligently brought into orderly activity, the power of our thought will spend its uncontrolled forces in devastating energy, tearing apart all the resources that could have been used constructively.

This is nothing exceptional; it's merely the reappearance of the same principle that pervades all the forces of Nature. Think about it: which of these is not destructive unless drawn off into some definite direction? Accumulated steam, accumulated electricity, accumulated water, will at length burst forth, carrying destruction all around; but, drawn off through suitable channels, they become sources of constructive power, inexhaustible as Nature itself.

Fortunately, many causes are operating to give direction to humanity's otherwise unregulated thoughts, even when the thinkers themselves are ignorant of what thought-power is. This means that any ill effects of wrongly directed thought are mitigated somewhat. But even with these aids, the general stream of unregulated thought must have an adverse tendency, leading to an overall degradation of the human experience over time.

Accumulating Power

And here let me pause to draw attention to this idea of accumulation. The greater the accumulation of energy, the greater the danger if it is not properly directed, and the greater the power when it is directed. Fortunately for humanity the physical forces, such as electricity, are not usually found in a highly concentrated form. Occasionally circumstances produce such concentration, as in lightning, or at a power plant, but as a rule the elements of power are more or less equally dispersed.

Similarly, for the mass of humanity, our spiritual power has not yet reached a very high degree of concentration. Every mind, it is true, must be in some measure a center of concentration in order to experience conscious individuality, but most of humanity is not trained to focus the mind beyond that.

The power of the individualized mind rises rapidly, however, as it recognizes its unity with the infinite Life of Universal Spirit, and Its thought-currents then assume a proportionately greater significance. Whether well- or ill-directed, they have a measurable effect on their environment.[19]

Hence the instructed mind seeks to free itself from the entanglements of disordered thought, and to help others to do the same.[20] Indeed, to provide upward direction to the thoughts of ignorant thinkers is the purpose of much religious teaching, which the many uninstructed ones must accept by their faith in someone else's authority until they are able to realize its true value. Ultimately, they will discover that to escape from the entanglement of unregulated thought is to attain perfect Liberty, which is perfect Power.

ESSENTIAL POINTS

- If a principle exists at all, it applies to spiritual nature as well as the material world; this is the doctrine of Continuity: there is not one law for the part and another for the whole, but the same law permeates both.
- Each of us is the center of our own universe, which extends out infinitely in all directions from our bodies, and we are constantly creating and developing the world around us through the energies of Thought and Motion.
- Each of us is also one of innumerable elements in a higher system, and this system is part of a higher system, which is part of a still higher system, ongoing until we reach the supreme center of all things.
- Recognizing that we are alive and have power in our world because we are part of something that functions

---

[19] To some extent this is the theme of Lynn Andrew's classic *Medicine Woman*. It is also the essence of David Hawkens' *Power vs. Force*.

[20] This is the goal of Buddhist practice, and what's called "the *boddhisatva* vow´: to learn to regulate the mind and to teach others how to, so all may be free.

with certainty gives us the freedom to use that power for our well-being, as long as it is also for the well-being of all others.

- Thoughts naturally and consistently produce an external effect, so we are continually creating for ourselves a world of surroundings which accurately reproduces our own thoughts.

- The power of the individualized mind increases rapidly as it recognizes its unity with Infinite Life, and the individual's thought-currents, whether well- or ill-directed, will have a greater effect on their environment.

- Hence the instructed mind frees itself from the entanglements of disordered thought, and helps others to do the same so that all may experience freedom and well-being.

Exercises

1. Discovering thoughts and their effects:
   a. Set aside a few times (about half an hour each) in the next week or so to simply watch your thoughts. They can be observed while you're doing any "mindless" task (like driving, washing dishes, working in the garden, working out, ironing, sitting in a relaxed state, or preparing to sleep, or, as Ram Das learned from a woman in one of his audiences, crocheting). Don't try to do anything with the thoughts that come up; simply observe them. If you're inspired or suddenly remember something, write it down and go back to the process you were in before. There's nothing to be done here, just the experience of observing what's going on in your mind.
   b. After you've done that a few times, sit down with a journal and do the same thing: sit quietly and observe your thoughts. Only this time, simply sit and rest your eyes on something, just breathing and writing down the thoughts that come up. Use abbreviations and whatever you need to catch the essence of a thought, then go back to your

breathing. Do this 3 - 4 times over a couple of weeks and see if the simple act of observation begins to change the nature of your thought.

   c. Get some graph paper or set up a spreadsheet, and make several different columns. The columns might be by subject matter—home, work, a project, a person, etc.—or by quality: loving, angry, fearful, happy, etc. Go back over your thought-journal and list your thoughts in each column.

   d. Now, consider: if my thoughts are creating my world, what kind of world are these thoughts creating?

2.   Directing thoughts for greater effect:

   a. Having observed what's going on in the mind, it's possible to begin to change it. The first step is to describe the world you'd like to be creating. So set aside an hour or so, take your journal, and write in it all the qualities of the world you'd like to be living in:

      i. the kind of people,

      ii. the kind of places,

      iii. the kind of activities, relationships, forms of beauty and joy, toys, tools,

      iv. the environments that would be "heaven" for you

      v. what would be your ideal life in an ideal world.

      vi. Repeat this several times over a week or so, refining and clarifying the description and lists in it.

   b. When you feel like you have a sense of what that ideal world would be, take the graph or spreadsheet you created in the previous exercise and set up another row or column. Now list, in that column, the thoughts that would create the kind of world you'd like to be living in. These are the thoughts that you want to be thinking in the future, now that you understand their power.

   c. Compare the list you've just created with the other thoughts in your table. In each column that includes thoughts that are not creating the world you want, write an alternative thought that would contribute to that world.

For example, you may have been thinking "my [coworker, spouse, sibling, friend] somehow manages to spoil everything we do together." That's not part of your ideal world, so you might write "my [coworker, spouse, sibling, friend] and I benefit from everything we do together."[21] That's more like how you want to be living, right?

d. Now, take the thoughts that you've written and practice them. Read them aloud, one by one, then let them sink in.
   i. How does your body feel when you think the original thought? The new thought?
   ii. If the new thought does not feel comfortable and relaxed, try to discover whether it's simply because it's new or because it isn't really in alignment with the kind of world you're creating. If it's not, then change it to come closer to your ideal.
e. Once you've selected your preferred thoughts, write them down on a card or piece of paper that you can carry with you. Now, as you're driving or working out or doing the dishes, or whatever, observe your thoughts, and whenever you start to think the original way, say "No. Not that." And replace it with the new thought that you've written down.
f. After a month (28 days, minimum) of practicing the replacing process, take some time with a journal and
   i. Observe your thoughts, writing them down.
   ii. Observe your world, writing down the ways it has come closer to your ideal.
   iii. There may be huge changes and will be tiny ones. Note them all, and ...
   iv. congratulate yourself on changing your world by changing your thoughts!

---

[21] If you consider it, both statements are true but the original statement focuses on your unhappiness over results that are different from what you expected, while the new statement (new thought) focuses on the long-term results: your learning through exposure to other ways of thinking and acting.

V. BECOMING FREE[22]

As described earlier, the entanglement from which we need to escape has its origin in the very same principle which gives rise to our liberty and power. It is the same principle, inverted.

Any sequence followed in an inverted order must produce an inverted result. In the simplest arithmetical form, if 10 divided by 2 equals 5, then 10 divided by 5 equals 2. The numbers are the same but the results are inverted. This goes a long way to explain many of the problems of life.

We often fall into the mistake of supposing that opposite results require opposite powers to produce them, but things become much simpler when we recognize that this is not the case;

the same power will produce opposite results when it starts from opposite poles.

The physical world affords endless examples of this. The dynamo or generator uses mechanical force to produce electricity, but invert this order and electricity is converted into the mechanical force of a motor — this going back and forth is what an alternator does in a car. First the rotation of a wheel produces electricity, and then, in the inverted sequence, electricity produces the rotation of a wheel. Accordingly, the inversion of

---

[22] from *The Hidden Power & Other Papers on Mental Science* #4

the same principle that gives us liberty and power creates the entanglement from which we need
to be delivered before power and liberty can be
attained.

The principle that "as a man thinks so he is"[23] is the
basic law of the human mind. It is the "*Cogito, ergo sum*
("I think — am aware — therefore I am"), Descartes starting point that I referred to earlier. Essentially, he's
telling us that if we trace all awareness to its basis we
find that it is all internal to us, all in our own minds,
purely subjective.

Our five senses would cease to exist were it not for
the subjective consciousness which interprets what
they communicate to it. Think about it: every mind
lives in a world that is given objective reality by its
own perceptions. The perceptions may be erroneous,
but they nevertheless constitute the reality of life for
the mind that gives form to them. I have seen a man
speak to the stump of a tree which in the moonlight
looked like a person standing in a garden, and repeatedly ask its name and what it wanted. So far as the
man's mind was concerned the garden contained a living man who refused to answer.

Thus

*no other life than the life we lead in our own mind
is possible.*

As a result, the advance of the whole species depends
on substituting new ideas of good, liberty, and harmonious order instead of their opposites *within our own
minds*. And this can be done only by having a good rea-

---

[23] From the Hebrew Bible, Proverbs 23:7, and James Allen's *As A
Man Thinketh,* updated in the Library of Hidden Knowledge volume *As
We Think, So We Are.*

son for accepting the new idea in place of the old. After all, we hold each one of our beliefs as truths or facts, and these beliefs can be changed only by discovering some reason for a different belief.

Cause and Effect

Now an infant's first perception of cause and effect is drawn from external observation only, so the child regards external acts as the only causes possible. Later, beginning to realize that many of his acts were harmful, immoral, or unlawful, and therefore deserve some form of retribution, the young person fears such retribution as the proper result of those actions.

Sadly, at this point, by reason of the fact that our minds have dominion over lesser systems — that "thoughts are things" and have an impact on our world — the evils which are feared take on form and plunge that person into adverse circumstances. This experience prompts further thoughts and actions that cause harm of some sort, and from these come a fresh crop of fears, which in their turn become externalized into fresh evils. Now a circle is formed from which there is no escape — as long as the person recognizes nothing but external acts as a causative power in the world.

This process is called many things; it's the Law of Works, the Circle of Karma, the Wheel of Fate. It's a process from which there appears to be no escape as long as we are human. It's the necessary law of things as they appear from external observation only; and, as long as the need for retribution remains a fundamental belief, each person's subjective consciousness makes it a reality for that person.

What is needed, therefore, is to establish the conception that external acts are NOT the only causative power, but that another causal principle is at work, namely that of pure thought. This is the law that builds faith, the law that allows liberty; it introduces us to a power which is able to set up a new sequence of causation, not affected by any past actions.

Continuity, not Retribution

But this change of mental attitude cannot be brought about until we have a reason for the change. We require some solid ground for our belief in this new, higher law. And, ultimately, we find that ground in the eternal relation between Spirit as it appears in the universal essence and in the particular experience.

When we realize that there really is nothing else but Spirit, and that we ourselves are individual expressions of the Intelligence and Love that rule the universe, then we have reached the firm ground we've been seeking for effective action.

In the old way of thinking the quality of thought was determined by the quality of the actions, and since those actions always fell short of perfection, the development of a higher thought-power was seen as impossible. In that system everything is seen from without looking in - action determining thought— which is an inverted order of process.

However,

in the true order of the universe, everything is seen from *within*. The thought determines the quality of the action; not *vice versa*.

Thought is free; it is at liberty to direct itself to the highest principles, which are then reproduced in outward activity.

This understanding takes us beyond the idea of duality as two opposites, into a different kind of a duality: the inner and the outer of the same unity. This is the polarity on the continuum of all Being that we discussed earlier.

We then realize that, because of this unity,

> our thought must have unlimited creative power and must be free to range where it will, in no way bound to accept as inevitable any consequences that might flow from our past actions.

Such would limit the illimitable.

In this realization the old sequence of Karma is cut off and a new, higher order has been introduced. The unity of Spirit is found to result in perfect Liberty for each individual, thus ensuring that right as inalienable.

The mind, through its own independent creative power, is, therefore, the way out of the fatal circle in which its previous ignorance had imprisoned it. People who achieve this understanding realize they are no longer bound by the consequences of former deeds, done in ignorance. In fact, they realize that

> they never were bound by consequences except so far as they gave those consequences power by false ideas of the truth.

Such people recognize we are free, that we are a "partaker of divine nature." They see that we do not lose our identity therein, but rather.

> we send forth our thought to produce any effect we choose, becoming more and more fully ourselves with an ever-expanding perfection, along a

line of development whose possibilities are inexhaustible.

Reconciliation

Clearly, not all humanity shares this knowledge. For the most part people still look upon God as an individual being outside themselves. The Spirit that the more instructed person understands to be unity of mind and identity of nature appears to others to be an externalized personalization of good and evil, dark and light, joy and suffering.

This is why most cultures contain the idea of a Messiah, or Savior. The idea is not, as some suppose, a misconception of the truth of Being. On the contrary, when rightly understood it implies the most complete grasp of that truth. Only supreme knowledge could inspire an idea that adapts to every level of mind so effectively. It's a translation of the relationship between the deepest laws of Being into terms that even the most unlearned can realize; a translation arranged with such consummate skill that, as the mind grows in spirituality, every stage of advance is met by a corresponding unfolding of its meaning.

And even the crudest understanding of the idea is sufficient for the entire renovation of an individual's thoughts. Even with the most childish notions about Divine justice being satisfied by the substitution of someone's life, the working result will be the same.

Those who accept the idea of a Savior guiding their lives can think of themselves as no longer bound by the law of retribution for past offenses, but as free to follow out a new law of Liberty as a child of God.

And, since the states of our subjective consciousness constitute the realities of our life, to *think* of oneself as free is to experience freedom, regardless of the logic used.[24]

With deeper understanding, some will find that the first explanation they learned of how it works was inadequate. If they can overcome the distaste for religion that too often follows that awareness, however, their further investigation will demonstrate, as we have seen, that our liberty has its roots in the eternal laws of Nature, which are never doubtful and can never be overturned.

Indeed, humanity's whole action has its root in the unchangeable laws of Universal Spirit expressing in and through our individual minds. And it is precisely for that reason that there is an ongoing need to offer something each of us can lay hold of as a sufficient ground for the life-giving change of mental attitude — whether that something be found in myth, in tradition, in science, or in the gospels. By that change alone can they be rescued from the fatal circle of entanglement that their own thoughts have been creating, as we discovered in the preceding chapter.

So, whatever our individual opinions may be as to the historical facts of Christianity, we shall find that the great figure of liberated and perfected humanity at its core fulfills the need of all humanity by setting forth the great ideal of divine power intervening to rescue humanity by becoming one with us. The concept is presented to us in some form in all religions, whether

---

[24] This has been demonstrated and stated over and over by people who have been imprisoned for their beliefs but say they never lost their freedom.

we accept it in the most literal sense or as a presentation of the deepest study of mental laws, or in
whatever variety of ways we may combine these two
modes of understanding.

The ultimate idea impressed upon the mind must
always be the same:

> there is a Divine process for knowing ourselves
> to be expressions of the creative Universal Spirit,
> as "children of God," and "partakers of the Divine
> nature."

Through that process we realize that there is solid
ground for *believing* ourselves free, and, as we have
seen, by force of this very belief we *become free.*

Freedom

The proper outcome of the study of the laws of
Spirit is not the gratification of a mere idle curiosity,
nor the acquisition of abnormal powers, but the attainment of our spiritual and emotional liberty.

When we have reached this goal, the old things
have passed away and all things become new.

> The old limitations are found to never have had
> any existence outside our own misconception of
> the truth,

and one by one they fall off as we advance into clearer
light.

When we have been made free by recognizing our
oneness with Infinite Being, we have ended the old series of sequences and are starting the new. The mystical
seven days of the old creation have been fulfilled, and
the first day of the new week dawns upon us with its
resurrection to a new life.

In this way the great doctrine of the octave[25], which ancient science traced through observations of Nature, and which modern science endorses (though ignorant of its supreme significance), is manifest. We leave one level of being and enter another, functioning at a higher level of vibration—the same note expressed at a higher level.

Realizing that the Life-Spirit we seek is *in ourselves*, our relation to all else becomes part of a wondrous, living, divine order in which every part works in harmony with the whole, and the whole in harmony with every part. It's a harmony as wide as infinity, in which there are no limitations save those embedded in the law of Love that is Universal Spirit: the need to act for the benefit of all.

Let the reader grasp firmly this one fundamental truth and the evolution of further truth from it is only a question of time:

> there is only One Spirit, however many forms it may be manifesting, and "the Unity of the Spirit is the Bond of Peace" among all beings.

ESSENTIAL POINTS

- The principle that "as a man thinks so he is"[26] is the basic law of the human mind.

---

[25] The eight notes on a piano (*do, re, mi, ...*) are a physical representation of a universal principle of harmony, reflected also in the 7-day week and the 7-year cycles of the Hebrew Bible.

[26] From the Hebrew Bible, Proverbs 23:7, and James Allen's *As A Man Thinketh*, updated in the Library of Hidden Knowledge volume *As We Think, So We Are*.

- Consciousness is all internal to us; our five senses would cease to exist were it not for the subjective consciousness which interprets what they communicate.

- Perceptions may be erroneous, but they nevertheless constitute the reality of life for the mind that gives form to them.

- In the old way of understanding the quality of thought was determined by the quality of external actions, and since those actions always fell short of perfection, the development of a higher thought-power was seen as impossible.

- In the true order of the universe everything is seen from *within*. The thought determines the quality of the action; not *vice versa*.

- Whatever our individual opinions may be as to the historical facts of Christianity, we shall find there the ultimate idea: there is a divine process for knowing ourselves to be expressions of Universal Spirit, "children of God", "partakers of the Divine nature".

- When we have been made free by recognizing our oneness with Infinite Being, we have ended the old series of action-and-consequence and are starting the new; the old limitations fall off as we realize they never have had any existence outside our own misapprehension of the truth.

- Realizing that the Life-Spirit we seek is *in ourselves*, our relation to all else becomes part of a wondrous, living, divine Order in which every part works in harmony with the whole, and the whole in harmony with every part.

- In this realization we are free, not losing our identity, but sending forth our thought to produce any effect we choose, becoming more and more fully ourselves with an ever-expanding perfection, along a line of development whose possibilities are inexhaustible.

Exercises

1. Set aside an hour or so and consider your life as a series of actions and consequences.
    a. Are there particular actions you felt you should be punished for? Were you?
    b. Are there times when you "got away with" something and feel some guilt?
    c. Are there experiences you've had that you, or someone around you, said "you must have done something bad to deserve this"?
2. Make a "mind map" of this section: on a large piece of paper, or white/black board, write the summary points in this chapter several inches apart and draw lines showing the relationships between them. Fill in experiences and other teachings you've encountered that support these ideas.
3. Take a sheet of paper and write the following statement at the top of the page: "I am an expression of Universal Spirit, creating my experience of an infinite universe with every thought."
    a. Now write all the reactions that come up around that idea—agreeing or disagreeing, arguing or supporting it
    b. Write the statement again
    c. Write everything that comes up again
    d. Repeat this sequence until what comes up is mostly agreeing, or you've identified a real sticking point for you... If you find some point you can't agree with do #2, above to resolve it.

VI. HEALING[27]

The subject of healing has been elaborately treated by many writers and fully deserves all the attention
that's been given to it, but our goal here is to ground
the reader in those general principles that underlie
the conscious use of the creative power of thought. I
will therefore examine the broad principles which appear to be common to the various methods of healing
by the mind.

Now the principle stated by all mental healers is
that

the appearance of illness is based in a belief and
the basis of all healing is a change in belief.

To recap what we've said thus far, the sequence from
which this understanding results is as follows:

1. the objective, aware mind impresses its thought
   upon the subjective, subconscious mind;
2. the subconscious or subjective mind is the creative faculty within us, and creates in the body
   and environment whatever thought is impressed upon it;

[27] from *The Hidden Power & Other Papers on Mental Science* #4

3. the thought is the expression of the belief;
4. this means that whatever the subjective mind creates is the external representation of our beliefs.

Accordingly, our whole object in healing is to change our beliefs.

To do this we need some solid ground of conviction of the falsehood of our old beliefs and of the truth of our new ones. This we find in the law of Causation. It can be stated as

Illness results from the belief that some material form or substance is a primary cause or entity that can cause disease or distress.

We know this belief to be false because our knowledge of Universal Spirit tells us that there is only one primary cause and it is that Spirit. We also know that the only true conception you can have of your essential self is as an extension of the pure, living Spirit, not hampered by conditions of any sort.

Your true, or absolute self, therefore, is not subject to illness.

Now, because the subconscious mind is directly linked with Universal Spirit, and accepts whatever it is told precisely as it is presented, it must externalize in our lives and world any idea that is firmly impressed upon it.

Applying this process to healing is not always successful at the first attempt, however, because all our life we have been holding the false belief in sickness as a primary cause, instead of merely a condition resulting from the true cause. This idea is, and must be, an idea planted in our subconscious mind, often during our earliest life experiences. And, in most cases, a belief which has become ingrained from childhood cannot be eradicated at a moment's notice.

We may find, therefore, that for some time after a treatment there is an improvement in the patient's health, and then, too often, the old symptoms return. This is because the new belief in one's own creative faculty has not yet penetrated down to the innermost depths of the subconscious mind, but has only partially entered it.

Elsewhere in these lectures I have pointed out the difference between placing an idea in the subconscious mind — that is, on the plane of the absolute, without reference to time and space — and placing the same idea in the conscious, intellectual mind, which only per-ceives things as related to time and space. In fact, a way to know that you are working at this level of mind is to experience the limitless state immediately before, or during, taking action. Then the new idea is most likely to take hold.

Each succeeding treatment strengthens the subcon-scious mind in its hold of the new belief, until at last a permanent cure is experienced. This is the method of self-treatment based on the patient's own knowledge of the law of his being.

But as was said of old, "there is not in all men this knowledge," or at any rate not such a full recognition of it as will enable them to give successful treatment to themselves. In these cases, the intervention of a healer becomes necessary.

The Process of Healing by Thought

The only difference between the healer and the patient is that the healer has learned how to control the less self-aware forms of Spirit by the more self-aware, while the patient has not. What healers do, then, is substitute their will, joined to their intellect, for that of the patient. In this way they can impress upon the patient's subconscious mind the suggestion of perfect health.

The question then arises, how can healers impress their own conscious mind on that of the patient? The answer shows the practical application of what we are calling New Thought.

Our ordinary conception of ourselves is that of an individual personality which ends at our skin, beyond which another personality begins, with the two personalities being entirely separate. This is an error.

> There is no hard and fast line between beings, and the boundaries between people (and with animals) can be increased or reduced by will.

In fact, those boundaries may be temporarily removed so completely that, for a time, the two personalities are merged into one.

A Mutual Process

Recognizing this, patients are asked by the healer to put themselves in a receptive mental attitude, to remove or reduce the barrier between their personalities so the mental power of the healer can enter. The healer does the same thing, except that while the patient withdraws the barrier with the intention of admitting a flowing-in, the healer does so with the intention of allowing a flowing-out.

Thus, by the joint action of the two minds, the barriers of both personalities are removed and the direction of the flow of intention is determined. It flows from the healer as actively willing to give, toward the patient as passively willing to receive. They thus follow the consistent law of Nature that the flow must always be from the plenum (fullness/positive) to the vacuum (emptiness/negative).

This process of mutual removal of the mental barrier between healer and patient is what is called "establishing rapport" between them.

As such, healing is a valuable practical application of the principle that pure Spirit is present in its entirety at every point throughout the universe, simultaneously. As soon as the healer realizes that the barriers of external personality have been removed, the healer can speak to the subconscious mind of the patient as if it were the healer's own. Realizing that both are Spirit, the healer's very thought of their identity in the Spirit makes them identical in Mind.

More, both minds are concentrated into a single entity at the single point on which the conscious mind of the healer can be brought to bear. This is in accordance with how thought works as a creative power in everyone: the control of the subjective mind by the objective mind through suggestion.[28]

You can see why, then, that it's so important to realize that each of us is Spirit. If we're seeing the human,

---

[28] This is precisely the mechanism that Phineas Parkhurst Quimby discovered and applied in the 1850s in Maine, and used it to heal thousands, including the then Mary Baker Patterson (later remarried to Asa Eddy). It was also why he often spoke harshly of ministers and doctors who, however unwittingly, set up a suggestive state in their listeners and then suggested that disease and distress would be their fate.

apparently diseased condition of the patient, we are thinking of a separate personality, not fixing our mind upon the pure Spirit that we both are — which is the one way we can enter and impress a true idea on our patient's essential, subconscious mind.

> We must therefore stop thinking about symptoms, and indeed about any personality or body altogether, and must think of this person as a purely spiritual individuality, in no way subject to any conditions.

More, we must realize the patient as an expression of Spirit choosing to manifest the vitality and intelligence that pure Spirit is.

The procedure continues, as follows.

1. Thinking of our patients in this way, we then affirm mentally that they are expressing outwardly that perfect vitality which we and they both know themselves to be their absolute state.
2. The patient's conscious thought is at the same time focused on receiving the active thought of the healer, so the patient's subconscious mind becomes thoroughly imbued with the recognition of its own life-giving power.
3. Then the patient's mind proceeds to work this suggestion out into external manifestation, and health is substituted for the apparent sickness.

It must be understood that the purpose of this process is to strengthen the subject's individuality, not to dominate it. To use it for domination is an inversion, which we have seen in our earlier exploration of Spirit's process brings its appropriate penalty to the operator.

Absent Healing Process

The above description describes the case where the patient is present with, and consciously co-operating with, the healer. In practice, it is in order to obtain this co-operation that the mental healer usually makes a point of instructing their patients in the broad principles of this Science of Spirit, if they are not already acquainted with them.

But this is not always advisable or possible. Sometimes stating principles that are opposed to the patient's existing prejudices arouses opposition, and any active antagonism on the patient's part must tend to intensify the barrier of conscious personality which the healer is aiming to remove. In these cases, absent treatment is effective.

If the reader has grasped all that has been said on the subject of spirit and matter, you will see that in mental healing treatments what we call time and space count for nothing. The whole action takes place in the subconscious, a plane unaffected by these limitations, and it therefore makes no difference whether the patient is in the immediate presence of the healer or in a distant country.

Experience has shown that, under these circumstances, one of the most effective modes of mental healing is by treatment during sleep, because then the patient's whole system is naturally in a state of relaxation which prevents any conscious opposition to the treatment. By the same rule the healer is also able to treat even more effectively during sleep than while waking.

The process is as follows:

1. Before going to sleep the healer repeats the
    statement and firmly impresses on his/her sub-
    jective mind that its job during the night is to
    convey curative suggestion to the subjective
    mind of the patient.
2. Then, by the general principles of the relation
    between subjective and objective mind this sug-
    gestion is carried out during the hours that the
    conscious individuality is shut down in sleep.

This method is applicable to young children to whom
the principles of the science cannot be explained as
well as persons at a distance.

Indeed, the only advantage gained by the personal
meeting of the patient and healer is in the instruction in
Spiritual Science that can be orally given, or when the
patient is at that early stage of knowledge where the
healer's visible presence conveys the idea that something is being done which could not be done in his
absence. Otherwise the presence or absence of the patient makes no difference.

The reader must always remember that the subconscious mind does not have to work through the
intellect or conscious mind to produce its curative effects; no thought is involved. The subconscious is part
of the all-pervading creative force of Spirit, while the
intellect is not at all creative, simply distributing the information it receives and processes.

Beyond Healing

From mental healing it is a short step to telepathy,
clairvoyance, and other manifestations of transcendental power. All of these are, from time to time, exhibited
by the subjective mind, and all of them follow laws as

accurate as those which govern what we are accustomed to see in the world around us.

The scope of this book, however, is not to explore psychic phenomena (experiences in that arena are described elsewhere[29]), but to lay down the broad principles which underlie all spiritual phenomena. Until these are clearly understood the student cannot profitably attempt the detailed study of the deeper powers. To attempt to do so without a firm foundation of knowledge and some experience in practical application would only be to expose oneself to unknown dangers. It would also be contrary to the scientific principle that advancing into the unknown can only happen from the known. To attempt otherwise brings us into a confused region of guess-work without any clearly defined principles for our guidance—which is the point at which we started, and, I do hope, have begun to untangle.

ESSENTIAL POINTS

- Because the subjective, or subconscious, mind creates whatever the objective, thinking mind impresses upon it, and since thought is the expression of belief, healing is little more than changing beliefs,.
- The belief that externalizes as sickness is the belief that some material condition is a primary cause or entity.
- Mental healing is not always successful the first time because we have been holding a false belief in sickness

---

[29] See Thomas Troward's *The Law and the Word* for his explanations of some of his own, personal "paranormal" experiences. See also the books, *Supernormal*, by Dean Radin, *The Science of the Paranormal*, by Lawrence LeShan, and *Frequency*, by Penney Peirce for some explorations of the scientific basis of such experiences.

as a cause, instead of a condition since childhood, which may not be eradicated in a moment.

- The only difference between the healer and the patient is that the healer has learned how to control the less self-aware forms of Spirit by the more self-aware, while the patient has not.

- Through the joint action of the two minds, the barriers between the personalities are removed and intention flows from the healer as actively willing to give, toward the patient as passively willing to receive.

- The healer can then speak to the subconscious mind of the patient as if it were the healer's own.

- In mental treatment time and space count for nothing; it therefore makes no difference whether the patient is in the presence of the healer or not.

- Mental healing during sleep works effectively with young children and also persons to whom the principles of the science cannot be explained.

- During sleep the patient's and healer's whole mental systems are naturally in a state of relaxation, so the subconscious mind does not have to work through the intellect or conscious mind to produce its curative effects.

- Before going to sleep the healer firmly impresses on his/her subjective mind that it is to convey curative suggestions to the subjective mind of the patient;

- this suggestion is carried out during all the hours that they both sleep.

- Mental healing is only one step away from a whole array of psychic phenomena which, like healing, must be studied from what is already known in the Science of Spirit to avoid confusion.

Exercises

1. Consider the last time you experienced symptoms of illness. Take a sheet of paper and write down what you were thinking:

    a. What did you tell yourself about it?
    b. What were people around you saying about illness?
    c. What were you thinking about your life situation? About religion and spirituality?

2. Consider the last time you went to a doctor, a therapist, or a practitioner. How receptive were you to what they were saying? Did you accept it without question? Did you do what they said without hesitation?

    a. Now consider what happened after that visit: did you immediately feel better? Did the symptoms return? If so, what were you thinking?
    b. What do you think might have happened if you had been in a different mode of consciousness — more receptive or less?

3. Take a sheet of paper and write down everything you think, feel, believe, or believe about physical and emotional distress, illness, sickness, or any form of discomfort.

    a. Ask yourself and write the answers for: Where does it come from? What causes it? How can it change? What does a person need to do to be free of it?
    b. Now re-read this section on Healing and write down what Troward says about illness, sickness, and discomfort of any kind. Do you believe what he says? What would it take for you to believe it?

4. Read other books about illness and healing such as the following:

    a. Louise Hay, *You Can Heal Your Life*

    b. Norman Cousins, *Anatomy of an Illness*
    c. Bruce Lipton, *Biology of Belief*
    d. Joe Dispenza, *You Are the Placebo*

VII. DEVELOPING OUR POWER[30]

Reviewing the Creative Process

In earlier chapters we have seen that the origin of the universe, and of the whole Creative Process, is the Self-contemplation in the void of a formless Intelligence that we have called Universal Spirit, and that the continuing contemplation of that Spirit's Self is the force or energy maintaining, evolving, and expanding all that is. We've seen that the process of Spirit contemplating Its Self continuously produces a reflection of whatever idea may be embodied in that contemplation, and in the manifestation of that idea as a form, which we call matter. And we've seen that there is a constant forward motion in Spirit's contemplation, and so of the matter that becomes manifest along the way.

Continuing this line of reasoning we found that the first reflection of the idea emerging from this Self-contemplation is a point of light that quickly expands and becomes a gas cloud or nebula, then progresses to the formation of the various contents of the universe, all the way to the emergence of human beings.

---

[30] from *The Hidden Power & Other Papers on Mental Science* #4

As we considered the nature of other forms and beings, it became clear that at the emergence of humans[31] the simple reproduction of that first idea comes to an end. We saw that up to, and including, genus *homo*, individual beings—plant, animal, and human—are what they are only by reason of the unconscious characteristics of their species and not by their exercise of individual, deliberate choice.

Moving Forward

As the process continues in its forward motion, the next step must necessarily be the emergence of individuals who are aware, as Spirit is, that they have the power to shape their own consciousness and environment. These individuals can see that

> the creative power of thought inherent in the Spirit that is expressing as their individualities enables them to take a conscious part in their own further evolution.

And on further reflection they can also see that the same creative power prevents any further evolution that is not harmonious with its own process.

So, in order to pass from the Fourth (mineral-vegetable-animal-human) kingdom into which we were born, to the Fifth (spiritual) Kingdom[32] that is our birthright, we need to understand the nature of our creative power and learn to work with it—not to inadvertently use it in a way that reduces our own and

---

[31] For those who consider that other self-aware beings exist in the universe, the term "human" here refers to all such.

[32] This shift, of human beings into the spiritual kingdom, is the focus of Henry Drummond's work, which is interpreted in the Library of Hidden Knowledge series under the title *One Law*.

others' capacity, but to be consciously intentional in enhancing our own and all others' well-being. And to do that, we need to understand that

the Creative Process works in only one way: by reciprocity, which could also be called reflection.

Drawing on the science of physics we might say that Spirit works by the Law of Action and Reaction, the reaction being always equivalent and correspondent to the action which generated it. We'll call this principle, the way that all things always work, the law of Reciprocity.

Once this law of Reciprocity is grasped, we can see how the forward movement of the Universal Spirit's creative process must result in producing a being who possesses the same power of independent spiritual initiative as Itself. That which it is contemplating is Its Self, and what it is contemplating shapes what is formed. It follows, then, that

the creative work of the whole that Spirit is must be continued within each single individuality.

To embody that awareness, then, people must learn to see that they possess this power, and then learn to see the most effective way to use it.

Not Just a Force of Nature

Doing so is not straightforward, though, because once we begin to open to the truth that we do possess this power, the temptation is to ignore the fact that our power is a product of the nature of the all-originating Spirit, rather than something unique to our person. Yet without being aware of the power's origin we could not see the greater life within which we live. We would never get nearer to it than the rest of those in the Fourth Kingdom stage, where the creative process is careful of the species, making sure it grows and develops, but careless of the individual, which may be lost in the process.

With such blind thinking we could never pass into the Fifth Kingdom, where the creative process is fully conscious and aware, at every level of being. We would miss the whole point of our transition to the more advanced mode of being, in which each individual consciously functions as a creative center for the unfolding of the world around them.

Without a universal power that works at a level higher than the genus or species, we would have to personally exercise our own inherent creative power. And in fact, that is precisely what most people in our society think. They believe that achieving various levels of success, or exercising what is generally called paranormal abilities, happens because of individual capacity rather than a simple reliance on the certainty of the principles by which Universal Spirit operates — in our lives, and in our world.

The Flow

Once we realize that our own power of creative initiative has its origin in the power of the All-Originating Spirit[33] then we see that there is a way to maintain the Spirit's life-giving energy in ourselves. That is, we can use our initiative in a way that impresses upon our

---

[33] This "similar faculty" that is in the Spirit and in us as individualizations of the Spirit is another way to think about the biblical passage "let us make man in our image." [Genesis 1:26]

subjective mind, which is our link with Spirit, the concept of our individual selves as relating to Universal
Spirit in a specific, individual, and personal way.

> We relate to Spirit in a way that takes us out of
> the mere category of *genus homo* and gives us a
> specific spiritual individuality of our own.

As we do so, our personal mental action produces
a corresponding reaction in the mind of the greater
Spirit, so that Spirit reproduces Itself as a special manifestation of Life in us. As long as this circulation
between the individual spirit and the Great Spirit continues, the individual's life is maintained, and even
strengthened.

It's strengthened because Spirit, as the original
Creative Power, is a multiplying force: any current sent
into it is not only reflected, but returned multiplied. So,
we may picture the multiplying tendency of the originating Mind taking our weak but clear thought and
multiplying it to higher and higher levels of power,
much as a transformer does with electricity. Then,

> the longer the circulation between the Mind of
> Spirit and the mind of the individual goes on, the
> stronger the individual mind becomes.

As this process becomes habitual and at last automatic,
each individual then experiences an endless flow of
Life, expanding their own mind in intelligence, love,
power and joy.[34]

At this point we must note carefully that all this
can *proceed only* from the individual's recognition that
our individual powers derive from the all-originating
Spirit. Also, we must understand that these powers can

---

[34] How to do this is laid out in Miller's book, *Uncommon Prayer.*

continue to be used constructively only as long as they are harmonious with the inherent forward movement of the Spirit: expanding the well-being of all beings.

The Inversion Effect

As we discovered earlier, any thought that is not in alignment with the Spirit's goodness — that is, benefitting all — must return to us as some form of distress. There must, therefore, be no inversion in the individual's self-image as presented to the originating power.

That very same Law by which we receive Life — the Law of reciprocal action and reaction — makes it so that every inversion we bring with us in presenting ourselves to the Spirit is bound to become our experience, as faithfully reproduced as our ideals might be. The stream of Pure Life is modified to fit our self-image, and it becomes less and less life-giving to the extent to which we invert its action by presenting an image of ourselves as less than we truly are. Even if that "less than" is a sense of unworthiness, poverty, lacking in any way, or as ill or handicapped, Spirit will accept it as what we intend and so reproduce it in our experience.

Similarly, the greater one's reliance on one's own personal power to employ spiritual forces, rather than relying on Spirit's power flowing through us, the less life-enhancing energy is supplied by Spirit. In extreme cases the stream flowing through and from the individual may even be rendered poisonous and deadly. Hence the belief in the power of "black magic" and "dark forces." But, deadly as those forces may be, their action must ultimately return to the person using them, and the life flowing to them must decrease with their use.

The existence of these distressing possibilities should never be overlooked, and therefore the essential condition for receiving the perfect fullness of Life is that we should present ourselves before the Universal Spirit free from every trace of inversion, from any idea that we are other than the pure expression of Spirit.

The Divine Ideal

And that means we must present ourselves in the likeness of a Divine Ideal, which only we, ourselves, can do. No one can do this for us. We must each project into the Eternal Mind a conception of our self as identical with its Eternal Ideal. If we can do this, then by the Law of Reciprocity, a return current will flow from the Eternal Mind reproducing this ideal with a continually growing power.

How are we to do this?

To induce this flow of Life individually we must first experience the conditions enabling us to do so in the universal. We can see this in physics as the principle that we can never create a force but can only use it in particular ways. Here, the power we want to use is the very power that leads to the formation of everything in the universe. Therefore, paradoxical as it may seem, we are required to have seen the universality of the specialized in order to specialize it for ourselves.

Now this is what all the spiritual traditions of the world offer in their stories and teachings. It is the essence of the Hindu *Bhagavad Gita*[35] and what the New

---

[35] Although on the surface the *Gita* is a war story, the dialogue is the explanation by Krishna, the Hindu incarnation of the divine, of how to experience all that unity with divinity offers.

Testament puts before us in its central figure, whom we call Jesus Christ.

Taking the gospel statements simply and literally, they show us a unique personality being the ideal principle of humanity in both spiritual origin and material manifestation. They portray the logical extreme of specialization in the embodiment of the universal Spirit and Substance. Thus, the New Testament sets the person we call Jesus Christ before us as the answer to whatever problem we're facing, and in this case, how to merge the special and the universal.

> If we fix our thought upon this unique personality as the embodiment of universal principles, it follows that those principles must come to exist in ourselves also.[36]

This means that the Christ's specialization of universal principles is the demonstration of our potential application of them. If we see this potential in ourselves as being identical with its manifestation in the Christ, then we can logically claim our identity with the Christ consciousness: what He has done we have done, what He is, we are.

If in this way we can recognize ourselves as identical with the Christ, then we present *this* image of ourselves to the eternal mind of Universal Spirit (the meaning of "I am the Way"). Then we bring with us no inverted conception to be reflected back, and import no negative currents into our particular stream of Life. This is what is meant by the phrase "in my name"[37],

---

[36] This principle is described in Troward's *The Hidden Power & Other Papers #4*, printed at the back of this book and interpreted as chapter IV. Applying the Principles, starting p 41.

[37] New Testament John 14:13-14

the word translated as "name", *shem* in Hebrew, meaning "nature, character".

This is how we reach "the Father" through "the Son." Holding ourselves in the image of the ideal, the Christ, allows us to "present ourselves faultless before the presence of the Divine glory with exceeding joy".[38] And the Spirit that is the original Creative Power flows that power easily through and as our individual selves.

This idea is not opposed to our modern science but is the culmination of all science, whether physical, mental, or spiritual. It is philosophical and logical throughout when you start the creative process in the only place it can start: the Self-contemplation of the Spirit in the void.

The gospel of "the Word made flesh"[39] is not, then, the meaningless cant of some petty sect, nor the cunning device of priestcraft—though it has been distorted in both these directions. Instead it is founded on the laws leading to the threefold nature of humanity, embracing the whole person—body, soul and spirit—as we have seen in earlier chapters.

The more carefully we examine the claims of the New Testament gospels the more we shall find that the Christ is indeed the mediator between God and Man, not by the arbitrary fiat of a capricious deity or priesthood, but by a logical law of sequence. In these stories, extremes meet, demonstrating that the Son of Man must also be the Son of God. When we see the reason why this is so, we receive power to become aware of

---

[38] Paraphrasing Jude: 24 in the New Testament epistles.
[39] Referring to the first verses of the gospel of John in the New Testament.

ourselves as children of God, or extensions of the Source of all.

We see then that we human beings are the *denouement* of the creative process in the Individual.

We are the point at which the Universal Spirit's contemplation begets individuals who can do the same.

This awareness explains another and important aspect of the gospels: the Christ's commission to His followers to heal the sick, which also follows logically from the law of the Creative Process, and the healing process, that we have explored in this text. Further, recognizing these great truths can affect the individual who has for a time put off its robe of flesh, appearing to no longer live, bringing back the sensation of vigor and life, once more.

It becomes clear then that, in the application of these principles, the Christ is the fulfilling of the Law. It also can be seen that "salvation," which may be most accurately defined as the fulfillment of our birthright (or, as the Buddhists call our life's plan, *dharma*), is not a silly shibboleth, and goes far beyond the limitations of a sacrifice on the cross. Rather it is the logical and vital process of our advance into the Fifth Kingdom, the next stage of the limitless capacities of our being.

The Secret

In all this, the great thing to bear in mind is that if a thing is true at all, there must be a reason why it is true. And

when we come to see the reasoning, we know the truth at first hand for ourselves and not from someone else's report. Then it becomes really our own and we begin to learn how to use it.

This is the secret of the individual's progress in any art, science, or business, and in seeking Life itself.

And it is why, as we apply the scientific method to move us forward on this great quest, we find that on every plane, the Way, the Truth, and the Life are ONE.

"A little philosophy inclineth a man's mind to atheism, but depth in philosophy bringeth men's minds about to religion."

~ Francis Bacon. *Essay xvi.*

ESSENTIAL POINTS

- The origin of the Universe is the Self-contemplation in the void of a formless Intelligence that we have called Universal Spirit, and Spirit's continuing Self-contemplation is maintaining, evolving, and expanding all that is.

- Up to and including genus *homo*, individuals are what they are only by reason of the unconscious characteristics of their species and not by their exercise of deliberate choice.

- As the creative process continues in its forward motion the next step must necessarily be the emergence of individuals aware that they are Spirit in expression and so have the power to shape their own consciousness and environment.

- Form can be thought of as the mineral, vegetable, animal, and human kingdoms — with fully aware individuals operating outside of space and time in a Fifth Kingdom.

- Following the Law of Reciprocation, our mental action produces a corresponding reaction in the mind of the Spirit, so that Spirit reproduces Itself as a special manifestation of Its Life in us in accordance with how we present ourselves in our relationship with It.

- To receive the perfect fullness of Life we must present ourselves before the Universal Spirit free from any trace of inversion of Its universal principles.

- Following the principle of Attraction, if we fix our thought upon the ideal embodiment of universal principles, those principles must come to exist in ourselves, and we can logically claim our identity with that embodiment, who is presented to us in all spiritual traditions, and in the New Testament as Jesus Christ.

- "Salvation" means the fulfillment of our life purpose (or, as the Buddhists call it, *dharma)*, and is therefore the process of our advance into the Fifth Kingdom, outside of space and time.

- When we come to see the reason for and know the truth at first hand it becomes really our own and we begin to learn how to use it;

- this is the secret of progress in any art, science, or business, and will serve equally well in our search after Life itself.

- As we move forward we find that on every plane the Way, the Truth, and the Life are ONE.

Exercises
1. Consider the creation story you were taught at school and/or in church.

    a. How does Troward's description fit?

    b. Can you find ways that it clearly disagrees or agrees?

    c. Can you see ways that his description makes sense of things that weren't explained by the other stories?

2. Remembering the earlier exercises, where you connected with the mind and spirit of other forms of being, explore the following:

    a. Which of the four kingdoms is this being a part of?

    b. Does Spirit express Itself in and through this being?

    c. Does this being know how to access the flow of Life of Spirit? To apply it in service to others?

3. Remember a time when you felt "in the flow," had all the energy you needed, and things went really well.

    a. What were the thoughts and feelings that preceded that experience? (often people feel it when they're "in love" or "wake up on the right side of the bed" or doing what they "were born to do.")

    b. What did you think about yourself, if anything, during and before that experience?

    c. Can you see any relationship between Troward's description of Spirit reciprocating our mental image in that experience?

4. Read about life in what Troward calls the Fifth Kingdom:

    a. Baird Spalding's *Life & Teaching of the Masters of the Far East*

    b. Jane Roberts' *Education of Oversoul 7*

    c. The *Bhagavad Gita*

    d. The gospels of the New Testament

5. Pay attention to your dreams and think about how things work in your dream worlds and learn about lucid dreaming as a way to live by choice instead of by instinct.

6. Consider the possibility of living in this lifetime outside of time and space:
    a. What would it feel like?
    b. What would you do?
    c. How would you be and do more than you are today?
7. Contemplate the universe as one whole, every part interconnected with and affecting every other part, across time and space, and beyond.
    a. Where are you in that whole?
    b. Where is Spirit?
    c. How does it feel to be the Spirit that pervades all that is?
    d. How does it feel to be constantly creating and discovering and becoming in an infinite range of forms?
    e. How is your individuality affected by this contemplation?

∞

SECTION TWO: ORIGINAL TEXTS

Following are the essays interpreted in the first half of this book, presented as originally written by Thomas Troward between 1904 and 1916. As with the other books in the Library of Hidden Knowledge series, we hope you will go back and forth between the two versions of the text, finding richer and deeper meanings as you do.

THE LAW AND THE WORD, CHAPTER 1

SOME FACTS IN NATURE

IF I WERE ASKED what, in my opinion, distinguishes the thought of the present day from that of a previous generation, I should feel inclined to say, it is the fact that people are beginning to realize that Thought is a power in itself, one of the great forces of the Universe, and ultimately the greatest of forces, directing all the others. This idea seems to be, as the French say, "in the air," and this very well expresses the state of the case—the idea is rapidly spreading through many countries and through all classes, but it is still very much "in the air." It is to a great extent as yet only in a gaseous condition, vague and nebulous, and so not leading to the practical results, both individual and collective, which might be expected of it, if it were consolidated into a more workable form. We are like some amateurs who want to paint finished pictures before they have studied the elements of Art, and when they see an artist do without difficulty what they vainly attempt, they look upon him as a being specially favoured by Providence, instead of putting it down to their own want of knowledge. The idea is true. Thought is the great power of the Universe. But to make it practically available we must know something of the principles by which it works—that it is not a mere vaporous indefinable influence floating around and subject to no known laws, but that on the contrary, it follows laws as uncompromising as those of mathematics, while at the same time allowing unlimited freedom to the individual.

Now the purpose of the following pages, is to suggest to the reader the lines on which to find his way out of this nebulous sort of thought into something more solid and reliable. I do not profess, like a certain Negro preacher, to "unscrew the inscrutable," for we can never reach a point where we shall not find the inscrutable still ahead of us; but if I can indicate the use of a screwdriver instead of a hatchet, and that the screws should be turned from left to right, instead of from right to left, it may enable us to unscrew some things which would otherwise remain screwed down tight. We are all beginners, and indeed the hopefulness of life is in realizing that there are such vistas of unending possibilities before us, that however far we may advance, we shall always be on the threshold of something greater. We must be like Peter Pan, the boy who never grew up—heaven defend me from ever feeling quite grown up, for then I should come to a standstill; so the reader must take what I have to say simply as the talk of one boy to another in the Great School, and not expect too much.

The first question then is, where to begin. Descartes commenced his book with the words "Cogito, ergo sum." "I think, therefore I am," and we cannot do better than follow his example. There are two things about which we cannot have any doubt—our own existence, and that of the world around us. But what is it in us that is aware of these two things, that hopes and fears and plans regarding them? Certainly not our flesh and bones. A man whose leg has been amputated is able to think just the same. Therefore it is obvious that there is something in us which receives impressions and forms ideas, that reasons upon facts and determines upon courses of action and carries them out, which is not the physical body. This is the real "I Myself." This is the Person we are really concerned with; and it is the betterment of this "I Myself" that makes it worth while to enquire what our Thought has to do in the matter.

Equally true it is on the other hand that the forces of Nature around us do not think. Steam, electricity, gravitation, and chemical affinity do not think. They follow certain fixed laws which we have no power to alter. Therefore we are confronted at the outset by a broad distinction between two modes of Motion—the Movement of Thought and the Movement of Cosmic Energy—the one based upon the exercise of Consciousness and Will, and the other based upon Mathematical Sequence. This is why that system of instruction known as Free Masonry starts by erecting the two symbolic pillars Jachin and Boaz—Jachin so called from the root "Yak" meaning "One," indicating the Mathematical element of Law; and Boaz, from the root "Awáz" meaning "Voice" indicating Personal element of Free Will. These names are taken from the description in I Kings vii, 21 and II Chron. iii, 17 of the building of Solomon's Temple, where these two pillars stood before the entrance, the meaning being that the Temple of Truth can only be entered by passing between them, that is, by giving each of these factors their due relation to the other, and by realizing that they are the two Pillars of the Universe, and that no real progress can be made except by finding the true balance between them. Law and Personality — these are the two great principles with which we have to deal, and the problem is to square the one with the other.

Let me start, then, by considering some well established facts in the physical world which show how the known Law acts under certain known conditions, and this will lead us on in an intelligible manner to see how the same Law is likely to work under as yet unknown conditions. If we had to deal with unknown laws as well as unknown conditions we should, indeed, be up a gum tree. Fancy a mathematician having to solve an equation, both sides of which were entirely made up of unknown quantities — where would he be? Happily this is not the case. The Law is ONE throughout, and the apparent variety of its working results from the infinite variety of the conditions under which it may work. Let us lay a foundation, then, by seeing how it works in what we call the common course of Nature. A few examples will suffice.

Hardly more than a generation ago it was supposed that the analysis of matter could not be carried further than its reduction to some seventy primary chemical elements, which in various combinations produced all material substances; but there was no explanation how all these different elements came into existence. Each appeared to be an original creation, and there was no accounting for them. But now-a-days, as the rustic physician says in Molière's play of the "Médecin Malgré Lui," "nous avons changé tout cela." Modern science has shown conclusively that every kind of chemical atom is composed of particles of one original substance which appears to pervade all space, and to which the name of Ether has been given. Some of these particles carry a positive charge of electricity and some a negative, and the chemical atom is formed by the grouping of a certain number of negatively charged particles round a centre composed of positive electricity around which they revolve; and it is the number of these particles and the rate of their motion that determines the nature of the atom, whether, for instance, it will be an atom of iron or an atom of hydrogen, and thus we are brought back to Plato's old aphorism that the Universe consists of Number and Motion.

The size of these etheric particles is small beyond anything but abstract mathematical conception. Sir Oliver Lodge is reported to have made the following comparison in a lecture delivered at Birmingham. "The chemical atom," he said, "is as small in comparison to a drop of water as a cricket-ball is compared to the globe of the earth; and yet this atom is as large in comparison to one of its constituent particles as Birmingham town-hall is to a pin's head." Again, it has been said that in proportion to the size of the particles the distance at which they revolve round the centre of the atom is as great as the distance from the earth to the sun. I must leave the realization of such infinite minuteness to the reader's imagination — it is beyond mine.

Modern science thus shows us all material substance, whether that of inanimate matter or that of our own bodies, as proceeding out of one primary etheric substance occupying all space and homogeneous, that is being of a uniform substance — and having no qualities to distinguish one part from another. Now this conclusion of science is important because it is precisely the fact that out of this homogeneous substance particles are produced which differ from the original substance in that they possess positive and negative energy and of these particles the atom is built up. So then comes the question: What started this differentiation?

The electronic theory which I have just mentioned takes us as far as a universal homogeneous ether as the source from which all matter is evolved, but it does not account for how motion originated in it; but perhaps another closely allied scientific theory will help us. Let us, then, turn to the question of Vibrations or Waves in Ether. In scientific language the length of a wave is the distance from the crest of one wave to that of the wave immediately following it. Now modern science recognizes a long series of waves in ether, commencing with the smallest yet known measuring 0.1 micron, or about 1/254,000 of an inch, in length, measured by Professor Schumann in 1893, and extending to waves of many miles in length used in wireless telegraphy — for instance those employed between Clifden in Galway and Glace Bay in Nova Scotia are estimated to have a length of nearly four miles. These infinitesimally small ultraviolet or actinic waves, as they are called, are the principal agents in photography, and the great waves of wireless telegraphy are able to carry a force across the Atlantic which can sensibly affect the apparatus on the other side; therefore we see that the ether of space affords a medium through which energy can be transmitted by means of vibrations.

But what starts the vibrations? Hertz announced his discovery of the electro-magnetic waves, now

known by his name, in 1888; but, following up the la-
bours of various other investigators, Lodge, Marconi
and others finally developed their practical application
after Hertz's death which occurred in 1894. To Hertz,
however, belongs the honour of discovering how to
generate these waves by means of sudden, sharply defined, electrical discharges. The principle may be
illustrated by dropping a stone in smooth water. The
sudden impact sets up a series of ripples all round the
centre of disturbance, and the electrical impulse acts
similarly in the ether. Indeed the fact that the waves
flow in all directions from the central impulse is one of
the difficulties of wireless telegraphy, because the message may be picked up in any direction by a receiver
tuned to the same rate of vibration, and the interest for
us consists in the hypothesis that thought-waves act in
an analogous manner.

That vibrations are excited by sound is beautifully
exemplified by the eidophone, an instrument invented,
I believe, by Mrs. Watts-Hughes, and with which I
have seen that lady experiment. Dry sand is scattered
on a diaphragm on which the eidophone concentrates
the vibrations from music played near it. The sand, as
it were, dances in time to the music, and when the music stops is found to settle into definite forms,
sometimes like a tree or a flower, or else some geometrical figure, but never a confused jumble. Perhaps in
this we may find the origin of the legends regarding
the creative power of Orpheus' lyre, and also the sacred
dances of the ancients — who knows!

Perhaps some critical reader may object that sound
travels by means of atmospheric and not etheric waves;
but is he prepared to say that it cannot produce etheric

waves also. The very recent discovery of transatlantic telephoning tends to show that etheric waves can be generated by sound, for on the 20th of October, 1915, words spoken in New York were immediately heard in Paris, and could therefore only have been transmitted through the ether, for sound travels through the atmosphere only at the rate of about 750 miles an hour, while the speed of impulses through ether can only be compared to that of light or 186,000 miles in a second. It is therefore a fair inference that etheric vibrations can be inaugurated by sound.

Perhaps the reader may feel inclined to say with the Irishman that all this is "as dry as ditch-water," but he will see before long that it has a good deal to do with ourselves. For the present what I want him to realize by a few examples is the mathematical accuracy of Law. The value of these examples lies in their illustration of the fact that the Law can always be trusted to lead us on to further knowledge. We see it working under known conditions, and relying on its unchangeableness, we can then logically infer what it will do under other hypothetical conditions, and in this way many important discoveries have been made. For instance it was in this way that Mendeléef, the Russian chemist, assumed the existence of three then unknown chemical elements, now called Scandium, Gallium and Germanium. There was a gap in the orderly sequence of the chemical elements, and relying on the old maxim—"Natura nihil facit per saltum"—Nature nowhere leaves a gap to jump over—he argued that if such elements did not exist they ought to, and so he calculated what these elements ought to be like, giving their atomic weight, chemical affinities, and the like; and when they were discovered many years later they were found to answer exactly to his description. He prophesied, not by guesswork, but by knowledge of the Law; and in much the same way radium was discovered by Professor and Madame Curie. In like manner Hertz was led to the discovery of the electro-magnetic waves. The celebrated mathematician Clerk-Maxwell had calculated all particulars of these waves twenty-five years before Hertz, on the basis of these calculations, worked out his discovery. Again, Neptune, the outermost known planet of our system was discovered by the astronomer Galle in consequence of calculations made by Leverrier. Certain variations in the movements of the planets were mathematically unaccountable except on the hypothesis that some more remote planet existed. Astronomers had faith in mathematics and the hypothetical planet was found to be a reality. Instances of this kind might be multiplied, but as the French say "à quoi bon?" I think these will be sufficient to convince the reader that the invariable sequence of Law is a factor to be relied upon, and that by studying its working under known conditions we may get at least some measure of light on conditions which are as yet unknown to us.

Let us now pass on to the human subject and consider a few examples of what is usually called the psychic side of our nature. Walt Whitman was quite right when he said that we are not all included between our hat and our boots; we shall find that our modes of consciousness and powers of action are not entirely restricted to our physical body. The importance of this line of enquiry lies in the fact that if we do possess extra-physical powers, these also form part of our personality and must be included in our estimate of our relation to our environment, and it is therefore worth our while to consider them.

Some very interesting experiments have been made by De Rochas, an eminent French scientist, which go to show that under certain magnetic conditions the sensation of physical touch can be experienced at some distance from the body. He found that under these conditions the person experimented on is insensible to the prick of a needle run into his skin, but if the prick is made about an inch-and-a-half away from the surface of the skin he feels it. Again at about three inches from this point he feels the prick of the needle, but is insensible to it in the space between these two points. Then there comes another interval in which no sensation is conveyed, but at about three inches still further away he again feels the sensation, and so on; so that he appears to be surrounded by successive zones of sensation, the first about an inch-and-a-half from the body, and the others at intervals of about three inches each. The number of these zones seems to vary in different cases, but in some there are as many as six or seven, thus giving a radius of sensation, extending to more than twenty inches beyond the body.

Now to explain this we must have recourse to what I have already said about waves. The heart and the lungs are the two centres of automatic rhythmic movement in the body, and each projects its own series of vibrations into the etheric envelope. Those projected by the lungs are estimated to be three times the length of those projected by the heart, while those projected by the heart are three times as rapid as those projected by the lungs. Consequently if the two sets of waves start together the crest of every third wave of the rapid series of short waves will coincide with the crest of one of the long waves of the slower series, while the intermediate short waves will coincide with the depression of one of the long waves. Now the effect of the crest of one wave overtaking that of another going in the same direction, is to raise the two together at that point into a single wave of greater amplitude or height than the original waves had by themselves; if the reader has the opportunity of studying the inflowing of waves on the seabeach he can verify this for himself. Consequently when the more rapid etheric waves overtake the slower ones they combine to form a larger wave, and it is at these points that the zones of sensation occur. If the reader will draw a diagram of two waved lines travelling along the same horizontal line and so proportioned that the crest of each of the large waves coincides with the crest of every third wave of the small ones, he will see what I mean: and if he then recollects that the fall in the larger waves neutralizes the rise in the smaller ones, and that because this double series starts from the interior of the body the surface of the body comes just at one of these neutralized points, he will see why sensation is neutralized there; and he will also see why the succeeding zones of sensation are double the distance from each other that the first one is from the surface of the body; it is simply because the surface of the body cuts the first long wave exactly in the middle, and therefore only half that wave occurs outside the body. This is the explanation given by De Rochas, and it affords another example of that principle of mathematical sequence of which I have spoken. It would appear that under normal conditions the double series of vibrations is spread all over the body, and so all parts are alike sensitive to touch.

I think, then, we may assume on the basis of De Rochas' experiments and others that there are such things as etheric vibrations proceeding from human personality, and in the next chapter I will give some examples showing that the psychic personality extends still further than these experiments, taken by themselves, would indicate — in fact that we possess an additional range of faculties far exceeding those which we ordinarily exercise through the physical body, and which must therefore be included in our conception of ourselves if we are to have an adequate idea of what we really are.

THE HIDDEN POWER & OTHER PAPERS ON MENTAL SCIENCE #2

WHAT, THEN, is this central principle which is at the root of all things? It is Life. But not life as we recognise it in particular forms of manifestation; it is something more interior and concentrated than that. It is that "unity of the spirit" which is unity, simply because it has not yet passed into diversity. Perhaps this is not an easy idea to grasp, but it is the root of all scientific conception of spirit; for without it there is no common principle to which we can refer the innumerable forms of manifestation that spirit assumes.

It is the conception of Life as the sum-total of all its undistributed powers, being as yet none of these in particular, but all of them in potentiality. This is, no doubt, a highly abstract idea, but it is essentially that of the centre from which growth takes place by expansion in every direction. This is that last residuum which defies all our powers of analysis. This is truly "the unknowable," not in the sense of the unthinkable but of the unanalysable. It is the subject of perception, not of knowledge, if by knowledge we mean that faculty which estimates the relations between things, because here we have passed beyond any questions of relations, and are face to face with the absolute.

This innermost of all is absolute Spirit. It is Life as yet not differentiated into any specific mode; it is the universal Life which pervades all things and is at the heart of all appearances.

To come into the knowledge of this is to come into the secret of power, and to enter into the secret place of Living Spirit. Is it illogical first to call this the unknowable, and then to speak of corning into the knowledge of it? Perhaps so; but no less a writer than St. Paul has set the example; for does he not speak of the final result of all searchings into the heights and depths and lengths and breadths of the inner side of things as being, to attain the knowledge of that Love which passeth knowledge? If he is thus boldly illogical in phrase, though not in fact, may we not also speak of knowing "the unknowable"? We may, for this knowledge is the root of all other knowledge.

The presence of this undifferentiated universal life-power is the final axiomatic fact to which all our analysis must ultimately conduct us. On whatever plane we make our analysis it must always abut upon pure essence, pure energy, pure being; that which knows itself and recognises itself, but which cannot dissect itself because it is not built up of parts, but is ultimately integral: it is pure Unity. But analysis which does not lead to synthesis is merely destructive: it is the child wantonly pulling the flower to pieces and throwing away the fragments; not the botanist, also pulling the flower to pieces, but building up in his mind from those carefully studied fragments a vast synthesis of the constructive power of Nature, embracing the laws of the formation of all flower-forms. The value of analysis is to lead us to the original starting-point of that which we analyse, and so to teach us the laws by which its final form springs from this centre.

Knowing the law of its construction, we turn our analysis into a synthesis, and we thus gain a power of building up which must always be beyond the reach of those who regard "the unknowable" as one with "not-being."

This idea of the unknowable is the root of all materialism; and yet no scientific man, however materialistic his proclivities, treats the unanalysable residuum thus when he meets it in the experiments of his laboratory. On the contrary, he makes this final unanalysable fact the basis of his synthesis. He finds that in the last resort it is energy of some kind, whether as heat or as motion; but he does not throw up his scientific pursuits because he cannot analyse it further. He adopts the precisely opposite course, and realises that the conservation of energy, its indestructibility, and the impossibility of adding to or detracting from the sum-total of energy in the world, is the one solid and unchanging fact on which alone the edifice of physical science can be built up. He bases all his knowledge upon his knowledge of "the unknowable." And rightly so, for if he could analyse this energy into yet further factors, then the same problem of "the unknowable" would meet him still. All our progress consists in continually pushing the unknowable, in the sense of the unanalysable residuum, a step further back; but that there should be no ultimate unanalysable residuum anywhere is an inconceivable idea.

In thus realising the undifferentiated unity of Living Spirit as the central fact of any system, whether the system of the entire universe or of a single organism, we are therefore following a strictly scientific method. We pursue our analysis until it necessarily leads us to this final fact, and then we accept this fact as the basis of our synthesis. The Science of Spirit is thus not one whit less scientific than the Science of Matter; and, moreover, it starts from the same initial fact, the fact of a living energy which defies definition or explanation, wherever we find it; but it differs from the Science of Matter in that it contemplates this energy under an aspect of responsive intelligence which does not fall within the scope of physical science, as such. The Science of Spirit and the Science of Matter are not opposed. They are complementaries, and neither is fully comprehensible without some knowledge of the other; and, being really but two portions of one whole, they insensibly shade off into each other in a borderland where no arbitrary line can be drawn between them. Science studied in a truly scientific spirit, following out its own deductions unflinchingly to their legitimate conclusions, will always reveal the twofold aspect of things, the inner and outer; and it is only a truncated and maimed science that refuses to recognise both.

The study of the material world is not Materialism, if it be allowed to progress to its legitimate issue. Materialism is that limited view of the universe which will not admit the existence of anything but mechanical effects of mechanical causes, and a system which recognises no higher power than the physical forces of nature must logically result in having no higher ultimate appeal than to physical force or to fraud as its alternative. I speak, of course, of the tendency of the system, not of the morality of individuals, who are often very far in advance of the systems they profess. But as we would avoid the propagation of a mode of thought whose effects history shows only too plainly, whether in the Italy of the Borgias, or the France of the First Revolution, or the Commune of the Franco-Prussian War, we should set ourselves to study that inner and spiritual aspect of things which is the basis of a system whose logical results are truth and love instead of perfidy and violence.

Some of us, doubtless, have often wondered why the Heavenly Jerusalem is described in the Book of Revelations as a cube; "the length and the breadth and the height of it are equal." This is because the cube is the figure of perfect stability, and thus represents Truth, which can never be overthrown. Turn it on what side you will, it still remains the perfect cube, always standing upright; you cannot upset it. This figure, then, represents the manifestation in concrete solidity of that central life-giving energy, which is not itself any one plane but generates all planes, the planes of the above and of the below and of all four sides. But it is at the same time a city, a place of habitation; and this is because that which is "the within" is Living Spirit, which has its dwelling there.

As one plane of the cube implies all the other planes and also "the within," so any plane of manifestation implies the others and also that "within" which generates them all. Now, if we would make any progress in the spiritual side of science—and every department of science has its spiritual side—we must always keep our minds fixed upon this "innermost within" which contains the potential of all outward manifestation, the "fourth dimension" which generates the cube; and our common forms of speech show how intuitively we do this. We speak of the spirit in which an act is done, of entering into the spirit of a game, of the spirit of the time, and so on. Everywhere our intuition points out the spirit as the true essence of things; and it is only when we commence arguing about them from without, instead of from within, that our true perception of their nature is lost.

The scientific study of spirit consists in following up intelligently and according to definite method the same principle that now only flashes upon us at intervals fitfully and vaguely. When we once realise that this universal and unlimited power of spirit is at the root of all things and of ourselves also, then we have obtained the key to the whole position; and, however far we may carry our studies in spiritual science, we shall nowhere find anything else but particular developments of this one universal principle. "The Kingdom of   Heaven   is   within   you."

THE HIDDEN POWER & OTHER PAPERS ON MENTAL SCIENCE #3

I HAVE LAID STRESS on the fact that the "inner-most within" of all things is Living Spirit, and that the Science of Spirit is distinguished from the Science of Matter in that it contemplates Energy under an aspect of responsive intelligence which does not fall within the scope of physical science, as such. These are the two great points to lay hold of if we would retain a clear idea of spiritual science, and not be misled by arguments drawn from the physical side of Science only — the livingness of the originating principle which is at the heart of all things, and its intelligent and responsive nature. Its livingness is patent to our observation, at any rate from the point where we recognise it in the vegetable kingdom; but its intelligence and responsiveness are not, perhaps, at once so obvious. Nevertheless, a little thought will soon lead us to recognise this also.

No one can deny that there is an intelligent order throughout all nature, for it requires the highest intelligence of our most highly-trained minds to follow the steps of this universal intelligence which is always in advance of them. The more deeply we investigate the world we live in, the more clear it must become to us that all our science is the translation into words or numerical symbols of that order which already exists. If

117

the clear statement of this existing order is the highest that the human intellect can reach, this surely argues a corresponding intelligence in the power which gives rise to this great sequence of order and interrelation, so as to constitute one harmonious whole. Now, unless we fall back on the idea of a workman working upon material external to himself—in which case we have to explain the phenomenon of the workman—the only conception we can form of this power is that it is the Living Spirit inherent in the heart of every atom, giving it outward form and definition, and becoming in it those intrinsic polarities which constitute its characteristic nature.

There is no random work here. Every attraction and repulsion acts with its proper force collecting the atoms into molecules, the molecules into tissues, the tissues into organs, and the organs into individuals. At each stage of the progress we get the sum of the intelligent forces which operate in the constituent parts, plus a higher degree of intelligence which we may regard as the collective intelligence superior to that of the mere sum-total of the parts, something which belongs to the individual as a whole, and not to the parts as such. These are facts which can be amply proved from physical science; and they also supply a great law in spiritual science, which is that in any collective body the intelligence of the whole is superior to that of the sum of the parts.

Spirit is at the root of all things, and thoughtful observation shows that its operation is guided by unfailing intelligence which adapts means to ends, and harmonises the entire universe of manifested being in those wonderful ways which physical science renders clearer every day; and this intelligence must be in the generating spirit itself, because there is no other source from which it could proceed. On these grounds, therefore, we may distinctly affirm that Spirit is intelligent, and that whatever it does is done by the intelligent adaptation of means to ends.

But Spirit is also responsive. And here we have to fall back upon the law above stated, that the mere sum of the intelligence of Spirit in lower degrees of manifestation is not equal to the intelligence of the complex whole, as a whole. This is a radical law which we cannot impress upon our minds too deeply. The degree of spiritual intelligence is marked by the wholeness of the organism through which it finds expression; and therefore the more highly organised being has a degree of spirit which is superior to, and consequently capable to exercising control over, all lower or less fully-integrated degrees of spirit; and this being so, we can now begin to see why the spirit that is the "innermost within" of all things is responsive as well as intelligent.

Being intelligent, it knows, and spirit being ultimately all there is, that which it knows is itself. Hence it is that power which recognises itself; and accordingly the lower powers of it recognise its higher powers, and by the law of attraction they are bound to respond to the higher degrees of themselves. On this general principle, therefore, spirit, under whatever exterior revealed, is necessarily intelligent and responsive. But intelligence and responsiveness imply personality; and we may therefore now advance a step further and argue that all spirit contains the elements of personality, even though, in any particular instance, it may not yet be expressed as that individual personality which we find in ourselves.

In short, spirit is always personal in its nature, even when it has not yet attained to that degree of synthesis which is sufficient to render it personal in manifestation. In ourselves the synthesis has proceeded far enough to reach that degree, and therefore we recognise ourselves as the manifestation of personality. The human kingdom is the kingdom of the manifestation of that personality, which is of the essence of spiritual substance on every plane. Or, to put the whole argument in a simpler form, we may say that our own personality must necessarily have had its origin in that which is personal, on the principle that you cannot get more out of a bag than it contains.

In ourselves, therefore, we find that more perfect synthesis of the spirit into manifested personality which is wanting in the lower kingdoms of nature, and, accordingly, since spirit is necessarily that which knows itself and must, therefore, recognise its own degrees in its various modes, the spirit in all degrees below that of human personality is bound to respond to itself in that superior degree which constitutes human individuality; and this is the basis of the power of human thought to externalise itself in infinite forms of its own ordering.

But if the subordination of the lower degrees of spirit to the higher is one of the fundamental laws which lie at the bottom of the creative power of thought, there is another equally fundamental law which places a salutary restraint upon the abuse of that power. It is the law that we can command the powers of the universal for our own purposes only in proportion as we first realise and obey their generic character. We can employ water for any purpose which does not require it to run up-hill, and we can utilise electricity for any purpose that does not require it to pass from a lower to a higher potential.

So with that universal power which we call the Spirit. It has an inherent generic character with which we must comply if we would employ it for our specific purposes, and this character is summed up in the one word "goodness." The Spirit is Life, hence its generic tendency must always be lifeward or to the increase of the livingness of every individual. And since it is universal it can have no particular interests to serve, and therefore its action must always be equally for the benefit of all. This is the generic character of Spirit; and just as water, or electricity, or any other of the physical forces of the universe, will not work contrary to their generic character, so Spirit will not work contrary to its generic character.

The inference is obvious. If we would use Spirit we must follow the law of the Spirit which is "Goodness." This is the only limitation. If our originating intention is good, we may employ the spiritual power for what purpose we will. And how is "goodness" to be defined? Simply by the child's definition that what is bad is not good, and that what is good is not bad; we all know the difference between bad and good instinctively. If we will conform to this principle of obedience to the generic law of the Spirit, all that remains is for us to study the law of the proportion which exists between the more and less fully integrated modes of Spirit, and then bring our knowledge to bear with determination.

THE HIDDEN POWER & OTHER PAPERS ON MENTAL SCIENCE #4

THE LAW OF SPIRIT, to which our investigation has now led us, is of the very widest scope. We have followed it up from the conception of the intelligence of spirit, subsisting in the initial atoms, to the aggregation of this intelligence as the conscious identity of the individual. But there is no reason why this law should cease to operate at this point, or at any point short of the whole. The test of the soundness of any principle is that it can operate as effectively on a large scale as on a small one, that though the nature of its field is determined by the nature of the principle itself, the extent of its field is unlimited. If, therefore, we continue to follow up the law we have been considering, it leads us to the conception of a unit of intelligence as far superior to that of the individual man as the unity of his individual intelligence is superior to that of the intelligence of any single atom of his body; and thus we may conceive of a collective individuality representing the spiritual character of any aggregate of men, the inhabitants of a city, a district, a country, or of the entire world.

Nor need the process stop here. On the same principle there would be a superior collective individuality for the humanity of the entire solar system, and finally we reach the conception of a supreme intelligence bringing together in itself the collective individualities of all the systems in the universe. This is by no means a merely fanciful notion. We find it as the law by which our own conscious individuality is constituted; and we find the analogous principle working universally on the physical plane. It is known to physical science as the "law of inverse squares," by which the forces of reciprocal attraction or repulsion, as the case may be, are not merely equivalent to the sum of the forces emitted by the two bodies concerned, but are equivalent to these two forces multiplied together and divided by the square of the distance between them, so that the resultant power continually rises in a rapidly-increasing ratio as the two reciprocally exciting bodies approach one another.

Since this law is so universal throughout physical nature, the doctrine of continuity affords every ground for supposing that its analogue holds good in respect of spiritual nature. We must never lose sight of the old-world saying that "a truth on one plane is a truth on all." If a principle exists at all it exists universally. We must not allow ourselves to be misled by appearances; we must remember that the perceptible results of the working of any principle consist of two factors—the principle itself or the active factor, and the subject-matter on which it acts or the passive factor; and that while the former is invariable, the latter is variable, and that the operation of the same invariable upon different variables must necessarily produce a variety of results. This at once becomes evident if we state it mathematically; for example, a, b or c, multiplied by x, give respectively the results ax, bx, cx, which differ materially from one another, though the factorx always remains the same.

This law of the generation of power by attraction applies on the spiritual as well as on the physical plane, and acts with the same mathematical precision on both; and thus the human individuality consists, not in the mere aggregation of its parts, whether spiritual or corporeal, but in the unity of power resulting from the intimate association into which those parts enter with one another, which unity, according to this law of the generation of power by attraction, is infinitely superior, both in intelligence and power, to any less fully integrated mode of spirit. Thus a natural principle, common alike to physical and spiritual law, fully accounts for all claims that have ever been made for the creative power of our thought over all things that come within the circle of our own particular life. Thus it is that each man is the centre of his own universe, and has the power, by directing his own thought, to control all things therein.

But, as I have said above, there is no reason why this principle should not be recognised as expanding from the individual until it embraces the entire universe. Each man, as the centre of his own world, is himself centred in a higher system in which he is only one of innumerable similar atoms, and this system again in a higher until we reach the supreme centre of all things; intelligence and power increase from centre to centre in a ratio rising with inconceivable rapidity, according to the law we are now investigating, until they culminate in illimitable intelligence and power commensurate with All-Being.

Now we have seen that the relation of man to the lower modes of spirit is that of superiority and command, but what is his relation to these higher modes? In any harmoniously constituted system the relation of the part to the whole never interferes with the free operation of the part in the performance of its own functions; but, on the contrary, it is precisely by means of this relation that each part is maintained in a position to discharge all functions for which it is fitted. Thus, then, the subordination of the individual man to the supreme mind, so far from curtailing his liberty, is the very condition which makes liberty possible, or even life itself. The generic movement of the whole necessarily carries the part along with it; and so long as the part allows itself thus to be carried onwards there will be no hindrance to its free working in any direction for which it is fitted by its own individuality. This truth was set forth in the old Hindu religion as the Car of Jagannath—an ideal car only, which later ages degraded into a terribly material symbol. "Jagannath" means "Lord of the Universe," and thus signifies the Universal Mind. This, by the law of Being, must always move forward regardless of any attempts of individuals to restrain it. Those who mount upon its car move onward with it to endlessly advancing evolution, while those who seek to oppose it must be crushed beneath its wheels, for it is no respecter of persons.

If, therefore, we would employ the universal law of spirit to control our own little individual worlds, we must also recognise it in respect to the supreme centre round which we ourselves revolve. But not in the old way of supposing that this centre is a capricious Individuality external to ourselves, which can be propitiated or cajoled into giving the good which he is not good enough to give of his own proper motion. So long as we retain this infantile idea we have not come into the liberty which results from the knowledge of the certainty of Law. Supreme Mind is Supreme Law, and can be calculated upon with the same accuracy as when manifested in any of the particular laws of the physical world; and the result of studying, understanding, and obeying this Supreme Law is that we thereby acquire the power to use it. Nor need we fear it with the old fear which comes from ignorance, for we can rely with confidence upon the proposition that the whole can have no interest adverse to the parts of which it is composed; and conversely that the part can have no interest adverse to the whole.

Our ignorance of our relation to the whole may make us appear to have separate interests, but a truer knowledge must always show such an idea to be mistaken. For this reason, therefore, the same responsiveness of spirit which manifests itself as obedience to our wishes, when we look to those degrees of spirit which are lower than our own individuality, must manifest itself as a necessary inflowing of intelligence and power when we look to the infinity of spirit, of which our individuality is a singular expression, because in so looking upwards we are looking for the higher degrees of ourself.

The increased vitality of the parts means the increased vitality of the whole, and since it is impossible to conceive of spirit otherwise than as a continually expanding principle of Life, the demand for such increased vitality must, by the inherent nature of spirit, be met by a corresponding supply of continually grow-

ing intelligence and power. Thus, by a natural law, the
demand creates the supply, and this supply may be
freely applied to any and every subject-matter that
commends itself to us. There is no limit to the supply of
this energy other than what we ourselves put to it by
our thought; nor is there any limit to the purposes we
may make it serve other than the one grand Law of
Order, which says that good things used for wrong
purposes become evil. The consideration of the intelligent and responsive nature of spirit shows that there
can be no limitations but these. The one is a limitation
inherent in spirit itself, and the other is a limitation
which has no root except in our own ignorance.

It is true that to maintain our healthy action within
the circle of our own individual world we must continually move forward with the movement of the larger
whole of which we form a part. But this does not imply
any restriction of our liberty to make the fullest use of
our lives in accordance with those universal principles
of life upon which they are founded; for there is not
one law for the part and another for the whole, but the
same law of Being permeates both alike. In proportion,
therefore, as we realise the true law of our own individuality we shall find that it is one with the law of
progress for the race. The collective individuality of
mankind is only the reproduction on a larger scale of
the personal individuality; and whatever action truly
develops the inherent powers of the individual must
necessarily be in line with that forward march of the
universal mind which is the evolution of humanity as a
whole.

Selfishness is a narrow view of our own nature
which loses sight of our place in relation to the whole,

not perceiving that it is from this very relation that our life is drawn. It is ignorance of our own possibilities and consequent limitation of our own powers. If, therefore, the evidence of harmonious correlation throughout the physical world leads irresistibly to the inference of intelligent spirit as the innermost within of all things, we must recognise ourselves also as individual manifestations of the same spirit which expresses itself throughout the universe as that power of intelligent responsiveness which is Love.

THE HIDDEN POWER & OTHER PAPERS ON MENTAL SCIENCE #5

THUS WE FIND ourselves to be a necessary and integral part of the Infinite Harmony of All-Being; not merely recognising this great truth as a vague intuition, but as the logical and unavoidable result of the universal Life-Principle which permeates all Nature. We find our intuition was true because we have discovered the law which gave rise to it; and now intuition and investigation both unite in telling us of our own individual place in the great scheme of things. Even the most advanced among us have, as yet, little more than the faintest adumbration of what this place is. It is the place of power. Towards those higher modes of spirit which we speak of as "the universal," the law of man's inmost nature makes him as a lens, drawing into the focus of his own individuality all that he will of light and power in streams of inexhaustible supply; and towards the lower modes of spirit, which form for each one the sphere of his own particular world, man thus becomes the directive centre of energy and order.

Can we conceive of any position containing greater possibilities than these? The circle of this vital influence may expand as the individual grows into the wider contemplation of his unity with Infinite Being; but any more comprehensive law of relationship it would be impossible to formulate. Emerson has rightly said that a little algebra will often do far more towards clearing our ideas than a large amount of poetic simile. Algebraically it is a self-evident proposition that any difference between various powers of x disappears when they are compared with x multiplied into itself to infinity, because there can be no ratio between any determinate power, however high, and the infinite; and thus the relation between the individual and All-Being must always remain the same.

But this in no way interferes with the law of growth, by which the individual rises to higher and higher powers of his own individuality. The unchangeableness of the relation between all determinate powers of x and infinity does not affect the relations of the different powers of x between themselves; but rather the fact that the multiplication of x into itself to infinity is mentally conceivable is the very proof that there is no limit to the extent to which it is possible to raise x in its determinate powers.

I trust unmathematical readers will pardon my using this method of statement for the benefit of others to whom it will carry conviction. A relation once clearly grasped in its mathematical aspect becomes thenceforth one of the unalterable truths of the universe, no longer a thing to be argued about, but an axiom which may be assumed as the foundation on which to build up the edifice of further knowledge. But, laying aside mathematical formulae, we may say that because the Infinite is infinite there can be no limit to the extent to which the vital principle of growth may draw upon it, and therefore there is no limit to the expansion of the individual's powers. Because we are what we are, we may become what we will.

The Kabbalists tell us of "the lost word," the word of power which mankind has lost. To him who discovers this word all things are possible. Is this mirific word really lost? Yes, and No. It is the open secret of the universe, and the Bible gives us the key to it. It tells us, "The Word is nigh thee, even in thy mouth and in thy heart." It is the most familiar of all words, the word which in our heart we realise as the centre of our conscious being, and which is in our mouth a hundred times a day. It is the word "I AM." Because I am what I am, I may be what I will to be. My individuality is one of the modes in which the Infinite expresses itself, and therefore I am myself that very power which I find to be the innermost within of all things.

To me, thus realising the great unity of all Spirit, the infinite is not the indefinite, for I see it to be the infinite of Myself. It is the very same I AM that I am; and this not by any act of uncertain favour, but by the law of polarity which is the basis of all Nature. The law of polarity is that law according to which everything attains completion by manifesting itself in the opposite direction to that from which it started. It is the simple law by which there can be no inside without an outside, nor one end of a stick without an opposite end.

Life is motion, and all motion is the appearance of energy at another point, and, where any work has been done, under another form than that in which it originated; but wherever it reappears, and in whatever new form, the vivifying energy is still the same. This is nothing else than the scientific doctrine of the conservation of energy, and it is upon this well-recognised principle that our perception of ourselves as integral portions of the great universal power is based.

We do well to pay heed to the sayings of the great teachers who have taught that all power is in the "I AM," and to accept this teaching by faith in their bare authority rather than not accept it at all; but the more excellent way is to know why they taught thus, and to realise for ourselves this first great law which all the master-minds have realised throughout the ages. It is indeed true that the "lost word" is the one most familiar to us, ever in our hearts and on our lips. We have lost, not the word, but the realisation of its power. And as the infinite depths of meaning which the words I AM carry with them open out to us, we begin to realise the stupendous truth that we are ourselves the very power which we seek.

It is the polarisation of Spirit from the universal into the particular, carrying with it all its inherent powers, just as the smallest flame has all the qualities of fire. The I AM in the individual is none other than the I AM in the universal. It is the same Power working in the smaller sphere of which the individual is the centre. This is the great truth which the ancients set forth under the figure of the Macrocosm and the Microcosm, the lesser I AM reproducing the precise image of the greater, and of which the Bible tells us when it speaks of man as the image of God.

Now the immense practical importance of this principle is that it affords the key to the great law that "as a man thinks so he is." We are often asked why this should be, and the answer may be stated as follows: We know by personal experience that we realise our own livingness in two ways, by our power to act and our susceptibility to feel; and when we consider Spirit in the absolute we can only conceive of it as these two modes of livingness carried to infinity. This, therefore, means infinite susceptibility. There can be no question as to the degree of sensitiveness, for Spirit is sensitiveness, and is thus infinitely plastic to the slightest touch that is brought to bear upon it; and hence every thought we formulate sends its vibrating currents out into the infinite of Spirit, producing there currents of like quality but of far vaster power.

But Spirit in the Infinite is the Creative Power of the universe, and the impact of our thought upon it thus sets in motion a veritable creative force. And if this law holds good of one thought it holds good of all, and hence we are continually creating for ourselves a world of surroundings which accurately reproduces the complexion of our own thoughts. Persistent thoughts will naturally produce a greater external effect than casual ones not centred upon any particular object. Scattered thoughts which recognise no principle of unity will fail to produce any principle of unity. The thought that we are weak and have no power over circumstances results in inability to control circumstances, and the thought of power produces power.

At every moment we are dealing with an infinitely sensitive medium which stirs creative energies that give form to the slightest of our thought-vibrations. This power is inherent in us because of our spiritual nature, and we cannot divest ourselves of it. It is our truly tremendous heritage because it is a power which, if not intelligently brought into lines of orderly activity, will spend its uncontrolled forces in devastating energy. If it is not used to build up, it will destroy. And there is nothing exceptional in this: it is merely the reappearance on the plane of the universal and undifferentiated of the same principle that pervades all the forces of Nature. Which of these is not destructive unless drawn off into some definite direction? Accumulated steam, accumulated electricity, accumulated water, will at length burst forth, carrying destruction all around; but, drawn off through suitable channels, they become sources of constructive power, inexhaustible as Nature itself.

And here let me pause to draw attention to this idea of accumulation. The greater the accumulation of energy, the greater the danger if it be not directed into a proper order, and the greater the power if it be. Fortunately for mankind the physical forces, such as electricity, do not usually subsist in a highly concentrated form. Occasionally circumstances concur to produce such concentration, but as a rule the elements of power are more or less equally dispersed. Similarly, for the mass of mankind, this spiritual power has not yet reached a very high degree of concentration. Every mind, it is true, must be in some measure a centre of concentration, for otherwise it would have no conscious individuality; but the power of the individualised mind rapidly rises as it recognises its unity with the Infinite life, and its thought-currents, whether well or ill directed, then assume a proportionately great significance.

Hence the ill effects of wrongly directed thought are in some degree mitigated in the great mass of mankind, and many causes are in operation to give a right direction to their thoughts, though the thinkers themselves are ignorant of what thought-power is. To give a right direction to the thoughts of ignorant thinkers is the purpose of much religious teaching, which these uninstructed ones must accept by faith in bare authority because they are unable to realise its true import. But notwithstanding the aids thus afforded to mankind, the general stream of unregulated thought cannot but have an adverse tendency, and hence the great object to which the instructed mind directs its power is to free itself from the entanglements of disordered thought, and to help others to do the same. To escape from this entanglement is to attain perfect Liberty, which is perfect Power.

THE ENTANGLEMENT from which we need to escape has its origin in the very same principle which gives rise to liberty and power. It is the same principle applied under inverted conditions. And here I would draw particular attention to the law that any sequence followed out in an inverted order must produce an inverted result, for this goes a long way to explain many of the problems of life. The physical world affords endless examples of the working of "inversion." In the dynamo the sequence commences with mechanical force which is ultimately transformed into the subtler power of electricity; but invert this order, commence by generating electricity, and it becomes converted into mechanical force, as in the motor. In the one order the rotation of a wheel produces electricity, and in the opposite order electricity produces the rotation of a wheel. Or to exhibit the same principle in the simplest arithmetical form, if 10 divided by 2 = 5 then 10 divided by 5 = 2. "Inversion" is a factor of the greatest magnitude and has to be reckoned with; but I must content myself here with only indicating the general principle that the same power is capable of producing diametrically opposite effects if it be applied under opposite conditions, a truth which the so-called "magicians" of the middle ages expressed by two trian-

gles placed inversely to one another. We are apt to fall
into the mistake of supposing that results of opposite
character require powers of opposite character to produce them, and our conceptions of things in general
become much simplified when we recognise that this is
not the case, but that the same power will produce opposite results as it starts from opposite poles.

Accordingly the inverted application of the same
principle which gives rise to liberty and power constitutes the entanglement from which we need to be
delivered before power and liberty can be attained, and
this principle is expressed in the law that "as a man
thinks so he is." This is the basic law of the human
mind. It is Descarte's "Cogito, ergo sum." If we trace
consciousness to its seat we find that it is purely subjective. Our external senses would cease to exist were it
not for the subjective consciousness which perceives
what they communicate to it.

The idea conveyed to the subjective consciousness
may be false, but until some truer idea is more forcibly
impressed in its stead it remains a substantial reality to
the mind which gives it objective existence. I have seen
a man speak to the stump of a tree which in the moonlight looked like a person standing in a garden, and
repeatedly ask its name and what it wanted; and so far
as the speaker's conception was concerned the garden
contained a living man who refused to answer. Thus
every mind lives in a world to which its own perceptions give objective reality. Its perceptions may be
erroneous, but they nevertheless constitute the very reality of life for the mind that gives form to them. No
other life than the life we lead in our own mind is possible; and hence the advance of the whole race depends

on substituting the ideas of good, of liberty, and of order for their opposites. And this can be done only by
giving some sufficient reason for accepting the new
idea in place of the old. For each one of us our beliefs
constitute our facts, and these beliefs can be changed
only by discovering some ground for a different belief.

This is briefly the rationale of the maxim that "as a
man thinks so he is"; and from the working of this
principle all the issues of life proceed. Now man's first
perception of the law of cause and effect in relation to
his own conduct is that the result always partakes of
the quality of the cause; and since his argument is
drawn from external observation only, he regards external acts as the only causes he can effectively set in
operation. Hence when he attains sufficient moral enlightenment to realise that many of his acts have been
such as to merit retribution he fears retribution as their
proper result. Then by reason of the law that "thoughts
are things," the evils which he fears take form and
plunge him into adverse circumstances, which again
prompt him into further wrong acts, and from these
come a fresh crop of fears which in their turn become
externalised into fresh evils, and thus arises a circulus
from which there is no escape so long as the man recognises nothing but his external acts as a causative
power in the world of his surroundings.

This is the Law of Works, the Circle of Karma, the
Wheel of Fate, from which there appears to be no escape, because the complete fulfilment of the law of our
moral nature today is only sufficient for today and
leaves no surplus to compensate the failure of yester-
day. This is the necessary law of things as they appear
from external observation only; and, so long as this

conception remains, the law of each man's subjective consciousness makes it a reality for him. What is needed, therefore, is to establish the conception that external acts are NOT the only causative power, but that there is another law of causation, namely, that of pure Thought. This is the Law of Faith, the Law of Liberty; for it introduces us to a power which is able to inaugurate a new sequence of causation not related to any past actions.

But this change of mental attitude cannot be brought about till we have laid hold of some fact which is sufficient to afford a reason for the change. We require some solid ground for our belief in this higher law. Ultimately we find this ground in the great Truth of the eternal relation between spirit in the universal and in the particular. When we realise that substantially there is nothing else but spirit, and that we ourselves are reproductions in individuality of the Intelligence and Love which rule the universe, we have reached the firm standing ground where we find that we can send forth our Thought to produce any effect we will. We have passed beyond the idea of two opposites requiring reconciliation, into that of a duality in which there is no other opposition than that of the inner and the outer of the same unity, the polarity which is inherent in all Being, and we then realise that in virtue of this unity our Thought is possessed of illimitable creative power, and that it is free to range where it will, and is by no means bound down to accept as inevitable the consequences which, if unchecked by renovated thought, would flow from our past actions.

In its own independent creative power the mind has found the way out of the fatal circle in which its previous ignorance of the highest law had imprisoned it. The Unity of the Spirit is found to result in perfect Liberty; the old sequence of Karma has been cut off, and a new and higher order has been introduced. In the old order the line of thought received its quality from the quality of the actions, and since they always fell short of perfection, the development of a higher thought-power from this root was impossible. This is the order in which everything is seen from without. It is an inverted order. But in the true order everything is seen from within.

It is the thought which determines the quality of the action, and not vice versa, and since thought is free, it is at liberty to direct itself to the highest principles, which thus spontaneously reproduce themselves in the outward acts, so that both thoughts and actions are brought into harmony with the great eternal laws and become one in purpose with the Universal Mind. The man realises that he is no longer bound by the consequences of his former deeds, done in the time of his ignorance, in fact, that he never was bound by them except so far as he himself gave them this power by false conceptions of the truth; and thus recognising himself for what he really is — the expression of the Infinite Spirit in individual personality — he finds that he is free, that he is a "partaker of Divine nature," not losing his identity, but becoming more and more fully himself with an ever-expanding perfection, following out a line of evolution whose possibilities are inexhaustible.

But there is not in all men this knowledge. For the most part they still look upon God as an individual Being external to themselves, and what the more instructed man sees to be unity of mind and identity of nature appear to the less advanced to be an external reconciliation between opposing personalities. Hence the whole range of conceptions which may be described as the Messianic Idea. This idea is not, as some seem to suppose, a misconception of the truth of Being. On the contrary, when rightly understood it will be found to imply the very widest grasp of that truth; and it is from the platform of this supreme knowledge alone that an idea so comprehensive in its adaptation to every class of mind could have been evolved. It is the translation of the relations arising from the deepest laws of Being into terms which can be realised even by the most unlearned; a translation arranged with such consummate skill that, as the mind grows in spirituality, every stage of advance is met by a corresponding unfolding of the Divine meaning; while yet even the crudest apprehension of the idea implied is sufficient to afford the required basis for an entire renovation of the man's thoughts concerning himself, giving him a standing ground from which to think of himself as no longer bound by the law of retribution for past offences, but as free to follow out the new law of Liberty as a child of God.

The man's conception of the modus operandi of this emancipation may take the form of the grossest anthropomorphism or the most childish notions as to the satisfaction of the Divine justice by vicarious substitution, but the working result will be the same. He has got what satisfies him as a ground for thinking of himself in a perfectly new light; and since the states of our subjective consciousness constitute the realities of our life, to afford him a convincing ground for thinking himself free, is to make him free.

With increasing light he may find that his first explanation of the modus operandi was inadequate; but when he reaches this stage, further investigation will show him that the great truth of his liberty rests upon a firmer foundation than the conventional interpretation of traditional dogmas, and that it has its roots in the great laws of Nature, which are never doubtful, and which can never be overturned. And it is precisely because their whole action has its root in the unchangeable laws of Mind that there exists a perpetual necessity for presenting to men something which they can lay hold of as a sufficient ground for that change of mental attitude, by which alone they can be rescued from the fatal circle which is figured under the symbol of the Old Serpent.

The hope and adumbration of such a new principle has formed the substance of all religions in all ages, however misapprehended by the ignorant worshippers; and, whatever our individual opinions may be as to the historical facts of Christianity, we shall find that the great figure of liberated and perfected humanity which forms its centre fulfils this desire of all nations in that it sets forth their great ideal of Divine power intervening to rescue man by becoming one with him. This is the conception presented to us, whether we apprehend it in the most literally material sense, or as the ideal presentation of the deepest philosophic study of mental laws, or in whatever variety of ways we may combine these two extremes. The ultimate idea impressed upon the mind must always be the same: it is that there is a Divine warrant for knowing ourselves to be the children of God and "partakers of the Divine nature"; and when we thus realise that there is solid ground for believing ourselves free, by force of this very belief we become free.

The proper outcome of the study of the laws of spirit which constitute the inner side of things is not the gratification of a mere idle curiosity, nor the acquisition of abnormal powers, but the attainment of our spiritual liberty, without which no further progress is possible. When we have reached this goal the old things have passed away and all things have become new. The mystical seven days of the old creation have been fulfilled, and the first day of the new week dawns upon us with its resurrection to a new life, expressing on the highest plane that great doctrine of the "octave" which the science of the ancient temples traced through Nature, and which the science of the present day endorses, though ignorant of its supreme significance.

When we have thus been made free by recognising our oneness with Infinite Being, we have reached the termination of the old series of sequences and have gained the starting-point of the new. The old limitations are found never to have had any existence save in our own misapprehension of the truth, and one by one they fall off as we advance into clearer light. We find that the Life-Spirit we seek is in ourselves; and, having this for our centre, our relation to all else becomes part of a wondrous living Order in which every part works in sympathy with the whole, and the whole in sympathy with every part, a harmony wide as infinitude, and in which there are no limitations save those imposed by the Law of Love.

I have endeavoured in this short series of articles to sketch briefly the principal points of relation between Spirit in ourselves and in our surroundings. This subject has employed the intelligence of mankind from grey antiquity to the present day, and no one thinker can ever hope to grasp it in all its amplitude. But there are certain broad principles which we must all grasp, however we may specialise our studies in detail, and these I have sought to indicate, with what degree of success the reader must form his own opinion. Let him, however, lay firm hold of this one fundamental truth, and the evolution of further truth from it is only a question of time — that there is only One Spirit, however many the modes of its manifestations, and that "the Unity of the Spirit is the Bond of Peace."

EDINBURGH LECTURES: ON HEALING

THE SUBJECT OF HEALING has been elaborately treated by many writers and fully deserves all the attention that has been given to it, but the object of these lectures is rather to ground the student in those general principles on which all conscious use of the creative power of thought is based, than to lay down formal rules for specific applications of it. I will therefore examine the broad principles which appear to be common to the various methods of mental healing which are in use, each of which derives its efficacy, not from the peculiarity of the method, but from it being such a method as allows the higher laws of Nature to come into play. Now the principle universally laid down by all mental healers, in whatever various terms they may explain it, is that the basis of all healing is a change in belief. The sequence from which this results is as follows : -- the subjective mind is the creative faculty within us, and creates whatever the objective mind impresses upon it; the objective mind, or intellect, impresses its thought upon it; the thought is the expression of the belief; hence whatever the subjective mind creates is the reproduction externally of our beliefs. Accordingly our whole object is to change our beliefs, and we cannot do this without some solid ground of conviction of the falsity of our old beliefs and of the truth of our new ones, and this ground we find in that law of causation which I have endeavoured to explain. The wrong belief which externalizes as sickness is the belief that some secondary cause, which is really only a condition, is a primary cause. The knowledge of the law shows that there is only oneprimary cause, and this is the factor which in our own individuality we call subjective or subconscious mind. For this reason I have insisted on the difference between placing an idea in the subconscious mind, that is, on the plane of the absolute and without reference to time and space, and placing the same idea in the conscious intellectual mind which only perceives things as related to time and space. Now the only conception you can have of yourself in the absolute, or unconditioned, is as purely living Spirit, not hampered by conditions of any sort, and therefore not subject to illness; and when this idea is firmly impressed on the subconscious mind, it will externalize it. The reason why this process is not always successful at the first attempt is that all our life we have been holding the false belief in sickness as a substantial entity in itself and thus being a primary cause, instead of being merely a negative condition resulting from the absence of a primary cause; and a belief which has become ingrained from childhood cannot be eradicated at a moment's notice. We often find, therefore, that for some time after a treatment there is an improvement in the patient's health, and then the old symptoms return. This is because the new belief in his own creative faculty has not yet had time to penetrate down to the innermost depths of the subconscious mind, but has only partially entered it. Each succeeding treatment strengthens the subconscious mind in its hold of the new belief until at last a permanent cure is effected. This is the method of self-treatment based on the patient's own knowledge of the law of his being.

But "there is not in all men this knowledge," or at any rate not such a full recognition of it as will enable them to give successful treatment to themselves, and in these cases the intervention of the healer becomes necessary. The only difference between the healer and the patient is that the healer has learnt how to control the less self-conscious modes of the spirit by the more self-conscious mode, while the patient has not yet attained to this knowledge; and what the healer does is to substitute his own objective or conscious mentality, which is will joined to intellect, for that of the patient, and in this way to find entrance to his subconscious mind and impress upon it the suggestion of perfect health.

The question then arises, how can the healer substitute his own conscious mind for that of the patient? and the answer shows the practical application of those very abstract principles which I have laid down in the earlier sections. Our ordinary conception of ourselves is that of an individual personality which ends where another personality begins, in other words that the two personalities are entirely separate. This is an error. There is no such hard and fast line of demarcation between personalities, and the boundaries between one and another can be increased or reduced in rigidity according to will, in fact they may be temporarily removed so completely that, for the time being, the two personalities become merged into one. Now the action which takes place between healer and patient depends on this principle. The patient is asked by the healer to put himself in a receptive mental attitude, which means that he is to exercise his volition for the purpose of removing the barrier of his own objective personality and thus affording entrance to the mental power of the healer. On his side also the healer does the same thing, only with this difference, that while the patient withdraws the barrier on his side with the intention of admitting a flowing-in, the healer does so with the intention of allowing a flowing-out: and thus by the joint action of the two minds the barriers of both personalities are removed and the direction of the flow of volition is determined, that is to say, it flows from the healer as actively willing to give, towards the patient as passively willing to receive, according to the universal law of Nature that the flow must always be from the plenum to vacuum. This mutual removal of the external mental barrier between healer and patient is what is termed establishing a rapport between them, and here we find one most valuable practical application of the principle laid down earlier in this book, that pure spirit is present in its entirety at every point simultaneously. It is for this reason that as soon as the healer realizes that the barriers of external personality between himself and his patient have been removed, he can then speak to the subconscious mind of the patient as though it were his own, for both being pure spirit the thought of their identity makes them identical, and both are concentrated into a single entity at a single point upon which the conscious mind of the healer can be brought to bear, according to the universal principle of the control of the subjective mind by the objective mind through suggestion. It is for this reason I have insisted on the distinction between pure spirit, or spirit conceived of apart from extension in any matrix and the conception of it as so extended. If we concentrate our mind upon the diseased condition of the patient we are thinking of him as a separate personality, and are not fixing our mind upon that conception of him as pure spirit which will afford us effectual entry to his springs of being. We must therefore withdraw our thought from the contemplation of symptoms, and indeed from his corporeal personality altogether, and must think of him as a purely spiritual individuality, and as such entirely free from subjection to any conditions, and consequently as voluntarily externalizing the conditions most expressive of the vitality and intelligence which pure spirit is. Thinking of him thus, we then make mental affirmation that he shall build up outwardly the correspondence of that perfect vitality which he knows himself to be inwardly; and this suggestion being impressed by the healer's conscious thought, while the patient's conscious thought is at the same time impressing the fact that he is receiving the active thought of the healer, the result is that the patient's subconscious mind becomes thoroughly imbued with the recognition of its own life-giving power, and according to the recognized law of subjective mentality proceeds to work out this suggestion into external manifestation, and thus health is substituted for sickness.

It must be understood that the purpose of the process here described is to strengthen the subject's individuality, not to dominate it. To use it for domination is inversion, bringing its appropriate penalty to the operator.

In this description I have contemplated the case where the patient is consciously co-operating with the healer, and it is in order to obtain this co-operation that the mental healer usually makes a point of instructing the patient in the broad principles of Mental Science, if he is not already acquainted with them. But this is not always advisable or possible. Sometimes the statement of principles opposed to existing prejudices arouses opposition, and any active antagonism on the patient's part must tend to intensify the barrier of conscious personality which it is the healer's first object to remove. In these cases nothing is so effective as absent treatment. If the student has grasped all that has been said on the subject of spirit and matter, he will see that in mental treatment time and space count for nothing, because the whole action takes place on a plane where these conditions do not obtain; and it is therefore quite immaterial whether the patient be in the immediate presence of the healer or in a distant country. Under these circumstances it is found by experience that one of the most effectual modes of mental healing is by treatment during sleep, because then the patient's whole system is naturally in a state of relaxation which prevents him offering any conscious opposition to the treatment. And by the same rule the healer also is able to treat even more effectively during his own sleep than while waking. Before going to sleep he firmly impresses on his subjective mind that it is to convey curative suggestion to the subjective mind of the patient, and then, by the general principles of the relation between subjective and objective mind this suggestion is carried out during all the hours that the conscious individuality is wrapped in repose. This method is applicable to young children to whom the principles of the science cannot be explained; and also to persons at a distance: and indeed the only advantage gained by the personal meeting of the patient and healer is in the instruction that can be orally given, or when the patient is at that early stage of knowledge where the healer's visible presence conveys the suggestion that something is then being done which could not be done in his absence; otherwise the presence or absence of the patient are matters perfectly indifferent. The student must always recollect that the subconscious mind does not have to work through the intellect or conscious mind to produce its curative effects. It is part of the all-pervading creative force of Nature, while the intellect is not creative but distributive.

From mental healing it is but a step to telepathy, clairvoyance and other kindred manifestations of transcendental power which are from time to time exhibited by the subjective entity and which follow laws as accurate as those which govern what we are accustomed to consider our more normal faculties; but these subjects do not properly fall within the scope of a book whose purpose is to lay down the broad principles which underlie all spiritual phenomena. Until these are clearly understood the student cannot profitably attempt the detailed study of the more interior powers; for to do so without a firm foundation of knowledge and some experience in its practical application would only be to expose himself to unknown dangers, and would be contrary to the scientific principle that the advance into the unknown can only be made from the standpoint of the known, otherwise we only come into a confused region of guess-work without any clearly defined principles for our guidance.

THE CREATIVE PROCESS IN THE INDIVIDUAL CHAPTER IX

WE ARE NOW IN A POSITION TO SEE the place occupied by the individual in the Creative Order. We have found that the originating and maintaining force of the whole Creative Process is the Self-contemplation of the Spirit, and that this necessarily produces a reciprocal corresponding to the idea embodied in the contemplation, and thus manifesting that idea in a correlative Form. We have found that in this way the externalization of the idea progresses from the condensation of the primary nebula to the production of human beings as a race, and that at this point the simple generic reproduction of the idea terminates. This means that up to, and including, genus *homo*, the individual, whether plant, animal, or man, is what it is simply by reason of species conditions and not by exercise of deliberate choice. Then we have seen that the next step in advance must necessarily be by the individual becoming aware that he has power to mold the conditions of his own consciousness and environment by the creative power of his thought; thus not only enabling him to take a conscious part in his own further evolution but precluding him from evolving any further except by the right exercise of this power; and we have found that the crux of the passage from the Fourth to the Fifth Kingdom is to get people so to understand the nature of their creative power as not to use it destructively.

Now what we require to see is that the Creative Process has always only one way of working, and that is by Reciprocity or Reflection, or, as we might say, by the law of Action and Reaction, the reaction being always equivalent and correspondent to the action which generated it. If this Law of Reciprocity be grasped then we see how the progress of the Creative Process must at length result in producing a being who himself possesses the power of independent spiritual initiative and is thus able to carry on the creative work from the stand-point of his own individuality.

The great crux is first to get people to see that they possess this power at all, and then to get them to use it in the right direction. When our eyes begin to open to the truth that we do possess this power the temptation is to ignore the fact that our power of initiative is itself a product of the similar power subsisting in the All-originating Spirit. If this origin of our own creative faculty is left out of sight we shall fail to recognize the Livingness of the Greater Life within which we live. We shall never get nearer to it than what we may call its generic level, the stage at which the Creative Power is careful of the type or race but is careless of the individual; and so at this level we shall never pass into the Fifth Kingdom which is the Kingdom of Individuality — we have missed the whole point of the transition to the more advanced mode of being, in which the individual consciously functions as a creative center, because we have no conception of a Universal Power that works at any higher level than the generic, and consequently to reach a specific personal exercise of

creative power we should have to conceive of ourselves as transcending the Universal Law.

But if we realize that our own power of creative initiative has its origin in the similar faculty of the All-
Originating Mind then we see that the way to maintain
the Life-giving energy in ourselves is to use our power
of spiritual initiative so as to impress upon the Spirit
the conception of ourselves as standing related to It in a
specific, individual, and personal way that takes us out
of the mere category of genus *homo* and gives us a specific spiritual individuality of our own. Thus our
mental action produces a corresponding re-action in
the mind of the Spirit, which in its turn reproduces itself as a special manifestation of the Life of the Spirit in
us; and so long as this circulation between the individual spirit and the Great Spirit is kept up, the individual
life will be maintained, and will also strengthen as the
circulation continues, for the reason that the Spirit, as
the Original Creative Power, is a Multiplying Force,
and the current sent into it is returned multiplied, just
as in telegraphy the feeble current received from a distance at the end of a long line operates to start a
powerful battery in the receiving office, which so mul-
tiplies the force as to give out a clear message, which
but for the multiplication of the original movement
could not have been done. Something like this we may
picture the multiplying tendency of the Originating
Mind, and consequently the longer the circulation between it and the individual mind goes on the stronger
the latter becomes; and this process growing habitual
becomes at last automatic, thus producing an endless
flow of Life continually expanding in intelligence, love,
power and joy.

But we must note carefully that all this can only proceed from the individual's recognition that his own powers are a derivative from the All-originating Spirit, and that they can continue to be used constructively only so long as they are employed in harmony with the inherent Forward Movement of the Spirit. Therefore to insure this eternally flowing stream of Life from the Universal Spirit into the individual there must be _no inversion_ in the individual's presentation of himself to the Originating Power: for through the very same Law by which we seek Life—the Life namely, of reciprocal action and re-action--every inversion we bring with us in presenting ourselves to the Spirit is bound to be faithfully reproduced in a corresponding re-action, thus adulterating the stream of Pure Life, and rendering it less life-giving in proportion to the extent to which we invert the action of the Life-principle; so that in extreme cases the stream flowing through and from the individual may be rendered absolutely poisonous and deadly, and the more so the greater his recognition of his own personal power to employ spiritual forces.

The existence of these negative possibilities in the spiritual world should never be overlooked, and therefore the essential condition for receiving the Perfect Fullness of Life is that we should present ourselves before the Eternal Spirit free from every trace of inversion. To do this means to present ourselves in the likeness of the Divine Ideal; and in this self-presentation the initiative, so far as the individual is consciously concerned, must necessarily be taken by himself. He is to project into the Eternal Mind the conception of himself as identical with its Eternal Ideal; and if he can do this, then by the Law of the Creative

Process a return current will flow from the Eternal Mind reproducing this image in the individual with a continually growing power. Then the question is, How are we to do this?

The answer is that to take the initiative for inducing this flow of Life individually it is a *sine qua non* that the conditions enabling us to do so should first be presented to us universally. This is in accordance with the general principle that we can never create a force but can only specialize it. Only here the power we are wanting to specialize is the very Power of Specialization itself; and therefore, paradoxical as it may seem, what we require to have shown us is the Universality of Specialization.

Now this is what the New Testament puts before us in its central figure. Taking the gospel statements simply and literally they show us this unique Personality as the Principle of Humanity, alike in its spiritual origin and its material manifestation, carried to the logical extreme of specialization; while at the same time, as the embodiment of the original polarity of Spirit and Substance, this Personality, however unique, is absolutely universal; so that the Bible sets Jesus Christ before us as the answer to the philosophic problem of how to specialize the universal, while at the same time preserving its universality.

If, then, we fix our thought upon this unique Personality as the embodiment of universal principles, it follows that those principles must exist in ourselves also, and that His actual specialization of them is the earnest of our potential specialization of them. Then if we fix our thought on this potential in ourselves as being identical with its manifestation in Him, we can logically claim our identity with Him, so that what He has done we have done, what He is, we are, and thus recognizing ourselves in Him we present *this* image of ourselves to the Eternal Mind, with the result that we bring with us no inversion, and so import no negative current into our stream of Life.

Thus it is that we reach "the Father" through "the Son," and that He is able to keep us from falling and to present us faultless before the presence of the Divine glory with exceeding joy (Jude 24). The Gospel of "the Word made flesh" is not the meaningless cant of some petty sect nor yet the cunning device of priestcraft, though it has been distorted in both these directions; but it can give a reason for itself, and is founded upon the deepest laws of the threefold constitution of man, embracing the whole person: body, soul and spirit. It is not opposed to Science but is the culmination of all science whether physical or mental. It is philosophical and logical throughout if you start the Creative Process where alone it can start, in the Self-contemplation of the Spirit. The more carefully we examine into the claims of the Gospel of Christ the more we shall find all the current objections to it melt away and disclose their own superficialness. We shall find that Christ is indeed the Mediator between God and Man, not by the arbitrary fiat of a capricious Deity, but by a logical law of sequence which solves the problem of making extremes meet, so that the Son of Man is also the Son of God; and when we see the reason why this is so we thereby receive power to become ourselves sons of God, which is the dénouement of the Creative Process in the Individual.

These closing lines are not the place to enter upon so great a subject, but I hope to follow it up in another volume and to show in detail the logic of the Bible teaching, what it saves us from and what it leads us to; to show while giving due weight to the value of other systems how it differs from them and transcends them; to glance, perhaps, for a moment at the indications of the future and to touch upon some of the dangers of the present and the way to escape from them. Nor would I pass over in silence another and important aspect of the Gospel contained in Christ's commission to His followers to heal the sick. This also follows logically from the Law of the Creative Process if we trace carefully the sequence of connections from the indwelling Ego to the outermost of its vehicles; while the effect of the recognition of these great truths upon the individuality that has for a time put off its robe of flesh, opens out a subject of paramount interest. Thus it is that on every plane Christ is the Fulfilling of the Law, and that "Salvation" is not a silly shiboleth but the logical and vital process of our advance into the unfoldment of the next stage of the limitless capacities of our being. Of these things I hope to write in another volume, should it be permitted to me, and in the meanwhile I would commend the present abstract statement of principles to the reader's attention in the hope that it may throw some light on the fundamental nature of these momentous questions.

The great thing to bear in mind is that if a thing is true at all there must be a reason why it is true, and when we come to see this reason we know the truth at first hand for ourselves and not from someone else's report--then it becomes really our own and we begin to learn how to use it. This is the secret of the individual's progress in any art, science, or business, and the same method will serve equally well in our search after Life itself, and as we thus follow up the great quest we shall find that on every plane the Way, the Truth, and the Life are ONE.

∞

BOOKS BY THOMAS TROWARD

The Edinburgh Lectures on Mental Science, 1904

The Dore Lectures on Mental Science, 1909

Bible Mystery and Bible Meaning, 1913

The Creative Process in the Individual, 1915

The Years 1914 to 1923 in Bible Prophecy, 1915

The Law and the Word, 1917

The Hidden Power and Other Papers on Mental Science, 1921

THE LIBRARY OF HIDDEN KNOWLEDGE[40]

As We Think, So We Are: James Allen's Guide to Transforming Our Lives

Natural Abundance: Ralph Waldo Emerson's Guide to Prosperity

The New Game of Life and How to Play It: Florence Scovel Shinn's classic, updated for modern readers

The New Master Key System: Charles Haanel's classic, updated for modern readers

The New Science of Getting Rich: Wallace Wattles' classic, updated for modern readers

One Law: Henry Drummond on Nature's Law, Spirit, and Love

The Spiritual Science of Emma Curtis Hopkins

---

[40] Published by Beyond Words/Simon & Schuster

OTHER BOOKS BY

RUTH L. MILLER

Coming Into Freedom: Emilie Cady's lesions in truth for the 21st century*

*Home: Creating A Future for Humanity^*

*Making the World Go Away: Thriving in End Times^*

*Mary's Power, embracing the Divine Feminine as the age of empire ends^*

The Paths of Power series—easy-to-read biographies of New Thought founders and teachers*

*The Science of Mental Healing: lives and teaching of New Thought teachers in America (updated and expanded edition of 150 Years of Healing)^*

Spiritual Success*

*Uncommon Prayer^*

*Unlocking the Power of the Secret: 10 Key Steps to transform your thoughts and life^*

Unveiling Your Hidden Power: Emma Curtis Hopkins' Metaphysics for the 21st Century*

---

* Published by Wisewoman Press
^ Published by Portal Center Press

OTHER TITLES FROM PORTAL CENTER PRESS

Awakening, a journey of enlightenment,
by Andree Cuenod

Butterfly Soup, changing your life from the inside out
by Aurora J. Miller

Empowered Care, mind-body medicine methods
by Robert Bruce Newman & Ruth L. Miller

Language of Life: answers to modern crises in an ancient way of speaking, *by Milt Markewitz & Ruth L Miler, with contributions by Batya Podos*

Miracles through Music, the odyssey of a Harpist Healer *by Joel Andrews*

Views from the Pew, moving beyond religion: discovering truth within, *by J C Pedigo and friends*

Wake UP! Our Old Beliefs Don't Work Anymore! *by Andree Cuenod*

…and fiction and spiritual explorations under the imprint
SPIRITBOOKS

CPSIA information can be obtained
at www.ICGtesting.com
Printed in the USA
LVHW041551010423
743158LV00001BA/172